LIVING SOCIOLOGY

EXERCISES TO TRAIN THE
SOCIOLOGICAL IMAGINATION

MICHAEL CARHART

Kendall Hunt
publishing company

Cover image © Shutterstock, Inc.

www.kendallhunt.com
Send all inquiries to:
4050 Westmark Drive
Dubuque, IA 52004-1840

Copyright © 2015 by Michael Carhart

ISBN 978-1-4652-7964-4

Printed in the United States of America

CONTENTS

INTRODUCTION

When I first began to teach, I assigned these little social experiments for my students to do on their own. This kind of thing often goes by the name of *ethnomethodology*, and it is a page taken straight out of the book of Harold Garfinkel.[i] My desire in assigning these social experiments was to allow for a more "hands on" approach in my life, classes, and pedagogy.

Many of the students were enthused to be able to do homework that allowed them to break a norm or two, and I kept receiving positive feedback on these social exercises. I originally started out with only a few, but as the reception grew, then I gradually added more. I now have roughly 30 or so exercises that the students and I perform outside of the classroom.

It seems to me that if we are to find out how we can use sociology in our everyday lives, then it necessarily follows that we need to start to learn how to practice it. Sociology, like so many other things in life, can really be a *way* of living.

THE NEED FOR THIS BOOK

For over a year now, I have been constantly asked by various students of mine to write down some explanations of the sociological exercises that I assign in my classes. Many of my students have been wondering how these exercises relate to the concepts that we study in class.

I originally sought to find a supplement text that could answer some of these questions for me. I am sorry to say that my search in this department came up shorthanded. The only book I was able to find (now out of print) is a book titled *The Un-TV and the 10 MPH Car* by author Bernard McGrane.[ii]

McGrane has been highly influential to me personally, and I drew inspiration from his book in order to help create some of these particular sociological exercises. He helped me see that we can really live this subject by practicing it. And through his encouragement, I attempted to implement this similar style in thinking in all my classes.

---

[i] Garfinkel, Harold. *Studies in Ethnomethodology*. New Jersey: Prentice-Hall, 1967. Print.
[ii] McGrane, Bernard. *The Un-TV and the 10 MPH Car*. California: The Small Press, 1994. Print.

McGrane helped his students develop something called *beginner's mind*. All that means is that we go into these exercises and try to see what we can see. No expectations. I originally tried his approach out for myself and found out that students without proper training in the discipline would just most likely walk away with only a funny story to tell. I found that many of them were unable to connect their experience with the subject of sociology! And this was a huge problem for me. Many of us are not trained to see these sociological concepts in our own experiences. Getting help to see the concepts is a job reserved for a practicing instructor teaching an *Introduction to Sociology* course.

It is along the lines of this practitioner attitude that I first began to use more structure in the exercises. I did this by giving students "signs" to look for when they performed the sociological exercises. I have found that with more of a guiding structure, the students can connect with the subject matter easily.

This little handbook has really been a long-term deliberation process of mine. It can help us to train in order to become better sociologists.

WHAT YOU WILL NEED

This book is designed to be an interactive reading experience. I feel the best kind of books always are. I am not going to ask you to read my particular thoughts on the subject matter and then do the exercises later. Please do them by yourself after you finish reading each chapter, and afterward try answering the questions as best as you can. And I cannot stress this enough, but this process is absolutely vital for getting anything out of this book.

My intention is to have you (the reader) practice sociology and understand some of its basic theories. I could not think of a better way to reinforce the understanding of these ideas than by the practice of reading, doing, writing, and answering questions. This dynamic process, I hope, will lead us all toward some key insights about how these theories have affected our lives.

I would ask that the reader please purchase a journal or notebook and a writing implement to go along with it.

In my classes, journal writing constitutes the bulk of the grade. Those of us who have practiced it for a long time have found it to be a great benefit in our lives. It has helped many of us gain insights into our own way of thinking and how we act. We are often surprised by what we write and also about how much we already actually understand about ourselves. Writing is an excellent way to explore self-knowledge. And as we will see soon enough, writing will become a refuge for exploring our experiences of the social world.

When we first begin to write in our journals, we will perform the chapter exercises and then afterward write down our experiences and answer a few focus questions (these question can be found at the end of each chapter).

Do not worry, the questions will not be difficult to answer nor will your reply to them take very long at all. I merely added them to help structure your experience of thinking sociologically. They are *necessary* for the whole enterprise, so please give them a real chance. And when you peruse the questions you can begin to get an understanding of what you should be looking for when you do each of the exercises.

Many of us who are new to the field might need a little help thinking in this brand new way. It is not very difficult to develop sociological thinking in our lives, but it will help us immensely if we have some kind of direction guiding us. This is why the focus questions have the real capacity to become our friend as we move through the book. I beseech you to remain close friends with the focus questions!

HOW TO READ

Let me pause briefly for a moment and say something about the necessary mood we should prepare to adopt as we continue reading this text.

We should not just sit down and theorize about our current situations in hopes that we might awaken some latent urge to "do" sociology. No, I find that it is more beneficial if we just spend time with the subject in other ways.

It has been my own observation that it is best to do only a small portion of reading and writing in a single sitting. Afterward, it is nice to just go out and practice the discipline itself with the exercises. I feel that when we first start practicing in this way, we should try and be gentle with ourselves or we may begin to develop hostile feelings toward the subject itself.

Think about it for a moment. And let us all be realistic with ourselves—most of us do not care about sociology the way our teacher does, and we may be taking this course in order to fill an elective. So this is not your first priority in life! I understand that, and that is one of the reasons why we are going to move at a slow pace and take it easy.

In my classes, I usually take it easy on the readings and assign a little bit at a time. I know there is a lot of material to cover in one semester, and only so much time to do it, but it would be a shame if all of us felt like we were just "going through the motions" together in the classroom. We should try our best to develop a friendship with the subject and the other people who are studying it with us, but all this comes only with the gentleness that I keep mentioning. If you are an instructor, then you have the double task of being gentle to yourself and others.

During my last semester, a student told me he personally enjoyed the small portion of readings that I assigned in class. He mentioned that since I assigned such small portions of reading, he could honestly find no excuse not to do it!

So start with a little bit of reading and balance it out with a little bit of writing. But make sure your reading is genuine. If you start to feel something as you read you may want to take a break and walk around or just sit down and think about what "moved" you. When you feel something during reading, it is always advisable to pause and linger in that feeling. I say this because that feeling often provokes real thinking toward the subject. Many of us miss this moment! We often fade away as we read. We may start out strong, but the portions are too long and we might be too uninterested in the material to give it a real shot. So make sure you read in small intervals. And remember, you are attempting to learn a new subject, so it might take you some time to gain interest in it. If we take it easy together as we approach the subject, then I feel that we will develop a nice lasting friendship with this new way of thinking.

THIS BOOK IS SET UP IN THREE PARTS

The book is designed to help the reader understand some of the basic theories in the discipline of sociology and some of the ways we can practice "seeing and doing" these theories within our lives.

As I mentioned before, the approach taken here is very "hands on" and therefore practical in its aim. I tried to make each exercise easy enough so that anyone could find the time to do it quickly during their busy schedules.

As for my writing style, I deliberately tried to write simple and explain the theories in a language that is nontechnical. This book is by no means an exhaustive treatment of each of the theories found here. For a more thorough treatment, I would advise you to look elsewhere.

Do not worry though, I will provide a reading list at the back of the book. The reading list will point you in the direction of some of the classics in the field and allow you a little space to explore them for yourself if you should wish to. I should also add that this book is not to be taken as an academic work in the sense of rigorous scholarship and citations. It is simply a practice manual for students and various readers from all walks of life who may have an interest in attempting to live a more sociological life. There are many ways to practice living life and what is provided here is only one way.

You can perform these exercises with friends, or if you are an instructor, you can ask students to do them for homework and take volunteers in class to share their personal experiences. This can be a very enriching experience for everyone involved. I speak from personal experience; I have noticed that it is a really a great way to get everyone in the class involved. When experiences are shared in a group setting, students feel like they may have something to contribute to the discipline, and this can only serve to encourage them further to read and think about the subject in a more enthusiastic manner.

As for the way each chapter is divided up. Each chapter has three sections and they are divided up as follows: a summarization of the theory and exercises, my own personal story doing the exercises, and a simple assessment section with some focus questions to answer. All of these sections interrelate and help build off each other to reinforce the central ideas of this book.

Summaries of the Main Idea and Exercises

I recommend reading the whole chapter once through before attempting any of these exercises. Many readers will be able to read through each chapter and immediately understand the theory. To further reinforce their comprehension, these readers will be able to create a strong memory by performing each of the exercises.

There are many of us, however, who will read through the chapter and still not understand what is being said. It may not be until we actually do the exercise that we begin to understand what is being said in the book. And this is just as good as well! One way of learning is not to be preferred to another. I would be very pleased if any of these available ways helped to bring about an understanding in the reader.

At the beginning of each chapter, I will briefly summarize the main ideas and exercises. I hope you enjoy this little summary of mine and find it to be rather handy. Everything is put up front so you can see what the main ideas are and the exercises that follow from them. As you read on, you will begin to see how the ideas and exercises work together in harmony to help us better understand the social world we live in.

You will also notice that I added short biographical blurbs throughout each of the chapters. As a sociological thinker gets name dropped in this book, I decided to add some context so that you are not completely lost. I also provided some of their most important works where many of these ideas can be located. If the reader should wish to go to the primary sources, then I totally support their quest!

It is also important to say right at the outset that sometimes these social experiments can take a somewhat dangerous turn. If you feel something is off or sense trouble coming on, then I would advise you to err on the side of caution and leave the experiment immediately.

Many of these exercises deal with violating *informal social norms*, and people can tend to have adverse reactions to this type of violation. Informal social norms are simply social rules that people follow and they often "go without saying."

So it is good to know when to end an experiment. I am thinking of times when security guards have approached me at a shopping center and demanded to know what I was doing. Whenever I felt like I was in trouble, I immediately abandoned the exercise. I usually let the person know that I am performing a social experiment; I think this tends to alleviate some of the tension.

If an intense moment like this happens to you, it can also be enlightening. After you walk away and report your experience in your journal, you can begin to see how strongly we identify with informal norms like these. The opposite may also be true. Many times when I have done these experiments nothing at all happened to me, but even *no results are results* in sociology! So be sure to record whatever happens.

My Story of the Sociological Exercise

I will provide in each chapter a brief story of my experience performing each of these exercises and how I was able to get a glimpse into some of the major ideas while doing it. The story will help provide a little context to the reader on how to do the exercise and some of what might happen when they do it.

This section can also help give you some encouragement when you are attempting to do these experiments on your own. It will help give you a little structure of what you might expect to find as you walk into each of these situations. With the help of the previous section, you can begin to see how theory and action play out together in our social lives, and upon seeing this, you can better understand your own social experience.

Assessment/Checklist/Questions

After the story, I will help give readers signs of what to look for and how this relates to the central ideas of the chapter.

At the end of the chapter, I will provide a brief checklist that is succinct in measure. This checklist will provide the highlights of the ideas and exercises. I provided this so I could give the reader a quick reference guide to peruse. I will also provide focus questions at the end of each chapter. When you go to perform the exercise, it is recommended that you consult the questions first, as they will help structure your experience sociologically. If we are not given any kind of structure at all, then we will be unable to know what we are supposed to be looking for. This whole book aims to become a basic training manual for living a more sociological life.

The Sociological Imagination

1

SUMMARY OF THE MAIN IDEA: SOCIOLOGICAL IMAGINATION

➤ The sociological imagination is thinking about your own culture and the historical social institutions that shape it.

➤ Culture is your story, experience, and ongoing practice of social life.

➤ Historical social institutions are nuanced patterns that develop throughout time and weave together to create a general purpose in society that shapes our lives. Often times, this purpose serves to give us limits within society.

SUMMARY OF THE MAIN EXERCISES: "DO NOTHING" & "VIEW FROM ABOVE"

➤ "Doing nothing"[i] is an exercise that is as easy as it sounds. Simply visit a public place, stand there for 10 minutes and see what happens.

➤ "View from above"[ii] is an exercise that helps us take a bigger approach to our thinking. Find a quiet spot that is free of distracting noises. Keep your eyes gently closed or you can choose to keep them open. If you keep them open, then just simply rest them on some object that is not too distracting. Imagine floating above yourself, so that you take an aerial view. Now imagine visiting the places that surround that area. See what is happening in those areas.

---

[i] McGrane, Bernard. *The Un-TV and the 10 MPH Car*. California: The Small Press, 1994. Print.
[ii] Hadot, Pierre. *Philosophy as a Way of Life*. Massachusetts: Blackwell Publishing, 1995. Print.

In many introductory sociology textbooks, we usually first encounter a basic concept that can help underscore our whole sociological endeavor. And it will set the tone and pace for the remainder of our journey. What we are talking about here is simply called the *sociological imagination,*[iii] and it was coined by a sociologist named C. Wright Mills circa 1958.

Sociological Thinker

C. Wright Mills (1916–1962)

Major Works: *Sociological Imagination* and *Power Elite*

    Mills was an American sociologist who used conflict theory in a time when functionalism was quite popular among academic sociologists. Conflict theory simply means that different interests among different social groups lead to conflict in society.

It might be helpful for us to ask ourselves at the outset, "what will it be like to develop this kind of imagination in our lives?" For starters, it seems to me that we ought to become more interested in our own daily lives. This seems to be the first step.

Please take a moment to consider where you are as you read this book. Politely excuse yourself from reading any further and take a moment to look around at your surroundings. Where are you at? Who is around you? What kinds of things are other people doing? These kinds of questions can help guide us into deeper insights about the society we live in. In sociology, we try our best to develop a real interest in what happens in our own lives and the lives of others. We do this by looking closely at our own lives and understanding how they interact with society around us.

I would like to point out that at first this can be a very difficult thing to do. Everyday happenings are usually very routine and may require no analysis. They can seem kind of boring and uninteresting to us. But on the other hand, this is also a very interesting insight. What seems so obvious to us usually does not need to be thought about, right? Please tell me, what is so obvious about any of this social stuff anyways?

Attempting to give our lives a second thought like that is one of the obstacles we might face on our sociological journey. To help us in our endeavor, we return to the question that we originally asked and this time we can ask it more directly: *what is the sociological imagination?*

Wherever you are right now, in the library, on a park bench, sitting at home, or lounging on your bed trying to keep yourself awake as you read this, you are in history and history is unfolding. Wherever you happen to be is where you can find your life.

The drama of society continues to unfold on the theater stage of life. Which scene are you in right now? Sociologists often think of people as actors. And the

---

[iii] Mills, C. Wright. *The Sociological Imagination.* New York: Oxford University Press, 1959. Print.

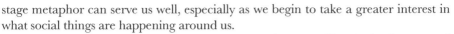

stage metaphor can serve us well, especially as we begin to take a greater interest in what social things are happening around us.

So these things are visible and highly personal to you. That is the first part of the definition of the sociological imagination. Your own story matters to you as you act out the drama of your social life. And all of us have our own stories that we tell each other.

We should also not forget the second part of the definition. It is a little more difficult to understand this part because it can be invisible to us. It seems that the ongoing saga of history continually affects our lives today in multifarious ways. Stories and ideas of long ago can remain hidden among us and affect our lives in ways that we might be unaware of.

Imagine what it was like before cellphones? There was a time when it would be impossible to reach someone at any time you pleased. Maybe to us now it seems absolutely irritating when someone forgets to bring their cellphone with them. It is a norm to have this device with us everywhere we go. But I digress, I just wanted to point out that a simple idea like this revolutionized our social experience in so many ways.

The sociological imagination is a way of thinking that continually asks us to reflect on our own lives and the larger forces in history which seem to shape them in various ways. This interconnected combination is something that we call *culture* and *social institutions*. Both of these terms and how they interconnect are the basic things that we tend to think about as sociologists.

Please allow me to provide an example that might help us better understand what these terms mean together. I am using a computer to write this book. How has the history and the creation of the computer affected my life as I currently write this book?

The history of the computer has affected the way I am writing the book because of its history. This logic seems somewhat circular, but history builds. This building process is what we call the structure of social institutions. There are many institutions that relate and connect to each other and affect our lives in various ways and we would do well to dwell on them from time to time.

In our example, there are many institutions that come together to affect the outcome of my life as I write this book. Among these institutions, a few include the economic, technological, academic, and political spheres. How do all of these spheres affect my life? This is where it can get a little tricky. Social institutions are not "objects" or physical things. Notice I said the "history of the computer" and not *a* computer (which I am currently using). In order to get an idea of what a social institution is, we need a little historical context. And we have to also think beyond what presents itself to us in the present moment.

I always think it is easier to introduce culture first, because it is more obvious to us. We live it and practice it. Going to the café and ordering a coffee is a cultural practice that seems so "natural" to us. The act often stands in no need of a second thought from us. I think it is important to say also that in this way culture helps hide social institutions.

It is hard to think about social institutions because they are not visible. How is it then that we know they are there? We can take measures to develop a way of seeing what is not visible. This, I think, is where the exercises are particularly helpful to us.

There is some kind of "force" that you will feel as you begin to violate informal norms. Remember norms are expectations each of us hold about what we think will happen in certain situations.

The first exercise we will perform can help us catch a glimpse of what a social institution is. Please go somewhere out in public and pause for 10 minutes. Just stand there without making a sound and "do nothing" as Bernard McGrane calls it. Go ahead and try it out for yourself right now.

Did you try it out for yourself? Did you feel that "force" that had you feeling like you were doing something wrong? That is a trace of a social institution that you were feeling.

Depending on where you are, you will feel different. When you are in a grocery store "doing nothing" you might feel out of place not moving or shopping. These kinds of places are centered on a purpose and generally people follow that particular purpose when they frequent it. Have you ever witnessed a person standing around doing nothing at a grocery store? If you have, you may have given that person a double take or a dirty look. What they were doing seemed somehow off to you. This is not your "moral compass" but your "normal compass" and it works to let you know when formal and informal norms are violated.

Essentially, what you are doing by violating the norm is breaking and freeing yourself of that institutional purpose. And believe me, there is something very liberating about that!

Also, this exercise can help us get some breathing room in our ordinary lives. As I mentioned previously, if we are too close to our lives, then we tend to take them for granted. When things become obvious to us, we do not think about them, but "obvious things" are exactly what sociologists think about. This is it! If you are not a fan of the obvious, then obviously you need to start to be!

When we begin to understand why "doing nothing" is so strange to do in society, we can find something out about the social world we live in. Why does it seem like we have to be constantly doing something in society? What does this say about the society we live in?

Another exercise that we can perform to help us further develop a sociological imagination and gain a perspective on social institutions is called "*the view from above.*"

This exercise was inspired by a French philosopher named Pierre Hadot. In his book *Philosophy as a Way of Life*, he talks about ancient philosophical schools which helped teach people how to live a good life. One of the exercises was to take a view from above. You were asked to imagine yourself floating above yourself and flying far away into the cosmos. This helped you to take a cosmic perspective on things. And it usually helped people see how small their problems really were in the grand scheme of things. Obviously, to use this exercise for our sociological purposes, I had to tweak it a bit. Instead of floating away into the vastness of the cosmos, I decided to take an aerial view of neighboring areas we happen to live around.

We can look at upper, middle, and lower class neighborhoods around the area we live in. We can also use this sociological imagination to look at different states, countries, or even time periods. It can be helpful to imagine New York in the 1950s. You might think it would be difficult to conjure all this up in our imagination, but it is not so hard. We just need a little bit of practice actually doing it.

I recommend doing this exercise every day for 5 minutes for the remainder of the course. When you do it, you can decide whether you want to focus on your region, a different time period, or another location. It is always best to start with what is familiar to you though, so please try and begin with the area you live at. I will forego telling a story of doing this particular exercise. I think what is crucial here is that we begin to "visit" areas that may be somewhat unfamiliar to us.

We need to be aware of what is going on in the world around us. Many of us live in one particular area and visit few places that are different from where we live at. If we cannot see that society is really *stratified*, then we are in some real danger. Taking a "view from above" can allow us to visit unfamiliar places that may need our attention and care, and we can see what is going on there. The more descriptive the trip, the better.

Our imagination is surprisingly fresh and vigorous. We need to only practice consistently every day in order to see real results in our lives. One of the benefits of this practice is the development of social compassion for others; a necessary attribute for doing good sociology.

If you are struggling with visualization, then please take the time to draw the area around you on paper. If drawing or visualization is not your forte, but you feel that words are, then please write a poem or two about this exercise. Simply take the time and give yourself some space to imagine how stratified society really is.

MY STORY OF "DOING NOTHING"

I have performed the "do nothing" exercise many times and in many places. I remember one particular day when the syllabus asked me to do this exercise for homework. I was not in the mood to cause a scene, as I was feeling somewhat under the weather, but like the good student that I am, I decided to go ahead with the experiment anyways.

I choose Marshall's as the site where I would do my homework. I thought I was clever because I decided to hang in the back of the store where the failed Home Goods items were. I figured no one would join me all the way back here. Many of the items were ridiculous looking, scattered, and half broken in a random mess. I found a little statue of Buddha to stare at and I set my cell phone alarm for 10 minutes.

I was enjoying the solitude for the first couple of minutes. I felt no social pressure at all. I was just kind of day dreaming in the aisle as my attention floated away. I did this until I realized that "day dreaming" was "doing something" and then I recalled my instructions for "do nothing."

This moment of peace and deliberation was, of course, very short lived. As you may know from experience yourself, the aisles in Marshall's are somewhat narrow.

Suddenly, somebody's grandma emerged from out of nowhere; she was on my left accompanied by an infant who was riding in the cart. She was rapidly approaching my direction and there was absolutely no way for her to get around me unless I moved. Soon I heard some words uttered to me in a kind tone, "Excuse me, sir." I never answered her back. How could I? My instructions were to do nothing, and talking means doing something! So I held my position in silence. Soon her tone turned from declarative statement to a more inquisitive one, "sir?"

I just kept standing there staring at the Buddha head. I tried to mimic the Buddha statue in its frozen glare. As you can already imagine, this was a very difficult thing to do. Every part of my being wanted to say "I am sorry" to her and move out of the way as quickly as possible.

Suddenly, I heard a yell to the right of me, "sir!" My peripheral vision told me it was a younger woman. Maybe it was the mother of that child? Or management? The words grew louder. Yes, I am now certain it was the mother.

In unison a chorus of "Sirs!" showered to my right and left. They were getting closer and closer to me and unrelenting. I kept thinking to myself that is a lot of "sirs!"

I felt that I was denying an essential part of myself. Usually, I dutifully follow many of the *informal norms* of society in public. Informal norms are expectations of behavior we may hold ourselves and others to, and when they get broken we may feel or respond adversely. In this case, I felt like I was playing the role of a jerk. I was becoming what I expected other people never to be to me.

In the middle of all this incessant noise, the baby began to cry. I looked into the Buddha statue's eyes and thought "Buddha, it seems like I am now the cause of a baby's tears and suffering! Which Noble Truth is this?"

It seemed like the whole social situation was about to reach a climax. The grandma and mother began to threaten to call security on me. They were scathing at this point and I was still utterly still in my nervous sweat. Swear words also began to surround me on both sides. Unimaginable swear words!

Shortly after the height of all this, they just decided to go around me. I was now left all alone in that aisle. No one was there anymore. I thought that they were probably going to grab security and come back. Another thought which I had was that I might have to abandon my post if security comes. And if they come, will I get in trouble for this whole thing? What if I am banned from this place? With these great deals all around me, where else would I go? And what did I even do? I was doing nothing, right?

My phone alarm went off. I came back to my senses and moved on. I immediately left Marshall's and sat in my car. All the social pressure seemed to dissolve. And I thought how strange it was that doing nothing can cause so much trouble for people!

Assessment/Checklist/Questions

Exercise 1: Instructions for "doing nothing" in society

- Pick a public place.
  - ○ Please make sure that public spot you choose is not a fire hazard or any other kind of hazard for that matter, that is, do not "do nothing" in the middle of a cross walk.
- Set an alarm on your phone or any other device for 10 minutes.
- Standstill and please do not talk to other people (even if they are talking to you).

- Notice any feelings and social pressures that might come up as you stand there.
- NOTE: If you feel or sense any kind of threat or danger, abandon the experiment immediately.

Exercise 2: *Instructions for the "view from above"*

- Find a quiet place where noise and distractions are minimal.
- Close your eyes or keep them open.
- Imagine yourself taking an aerial view above yourself.
- While in the aerial view, look around at the area you are currently at.
- When you feel comfortable enough, try and "fly" around to other places around the area, that is, go to upper, middle, and lower class areas.
- What are the people doing in each of the areas? What are they saying? How are they interacting? You can "zoom in" and listen to what is happening.
- If you are having trouble visualizing, you can draw the aerial view on paper and imagine that way. You can also write a poem or find some other creative way to get into this mood.

Focus Questions

- Write a list down of your cultural experience: from what you believe in, to what you wear, watch, to where you shop and live.
  - ○ Why do you think that the "doing nothing" and taking "a view from above" exercises can help us develop the sociological imagination?
- When you were in public "doing nothing," how did you feel?
  - ○ What do you normally do when you go to this particular public place?
  - ○ What were other people doing around you?
    - ■ Were you being stared at? Did you feel "judged?"
  - ○ Did you want to stop doing nothing and join everybody else?
  - ○ Were you approached by someone? If so, what happened?
  - ○ If norms are general expectations we have in society, what norms do you think you violated while doing this experiment?
    - ■ Start with basic shopping etiquette. How are you expected to act when you go to this place?
    - ■ Did you violate any particular values you personally hold?
- When you took the "view from above," what did you see?
  - ○ Where did you go? Be specific.
  - ○ How were the people behaving in these areas?
  - ○ What were they saying?
  - ○ How did the area look?
  - ○ Have you ever been to this area before?

Learning Social Methods

2

SUMMARY OF THE MAIN IDEAS: QUANTITATIVE & QUALITATIVE RESEARCH

➤ Quantitative research deals primarily with calculating the social world. This type of research will not be the focus of our attention in this book. Instead, we will aim to develop our qualitative methods. The style of this method deals with hanging out and observing people in a social environment and asking questions about it.

SUMMARY OF THE MAIN EXERCISES: UNOBTRUSIVE MEASURES & PARTICIPANT OBSERVATION

➤ When we practice unobtrusive measures,[i] we just hang back and watch what happens around us. This is also known as "people watching." As sociologists, when we watch what is happening around us, we usually look for certain things. These certain things will be highlighted by the questions at the end of this section.

➤ Participant observation is just like it sounds. We participant with the people and the environment around us by doing various things. We may begin by asking questions to other people. We could tell others that we are doing social research and ask if we can join their group if they would allow it. If we join in, we can observe as we participant with the group. It is worth noting that for any kind of successful research, it always helps to have a research question!

---

[i] Webb, Eugene J.; Campbell, Donald T.; Schwartz, Richard D.; Sechrest, Lee. *Unobtrusive Measures: Nonreactive Research in the Social Sciences.* Chicago: Rand McNally & Company, 1966. Print.

SUMMARY OF THE RESEARCH RULES

➤ Please do not do anything that might harm yourself or other people.

➤ Be honest with people and make your intentions known.

➤ Make sure you get their blessing to jot things down.

In this section, we will aim to develop some handy techniques that sociologists use in the field. This will help further aid us in using our sociological imagination as well as access key insights into our society.

There are an array of methods that sociologists use in order to help them understand society. I would like to focus on two methods in particular. If we practice both of these methods twice a week for the duration of a semester's time, then we will immediately see the benefits in our lives, and in turn, live our lives in a more sociological way.

In sociology, there are two branches of social research that we can use to help our sociological endeavor. The first branch is *quantitative research*. This is a branch that deals especially with calculation. We will not be focusing at all on this particular branch of research, but let me quickly say a few things about what it is.

Quantitative research involves learning how to speak the language of numbers in order to say something about the social world around us. This type of research can be very helpful to us but it usually involves some special training and a unified direction. We are just going to limit ourselves to learning the basic way of thinking sociologically.

Our branch of focus in this chapter will be *qualitative research.* This branch attempts to learn how to speak the language of relating socially with other people. This is also a vast area of study, so in order to narrow it down a little, we will look at two particular methods within it. These methods are *participant observation* and *unobtrusive measures*. It might be best for us to first begin with unobtrusive measures. Please allow me to briefly summarize what "unobtrusive measures" is.

Unobtrusive measures can also go by the name "people watching." It is a skill that many of us may already practice in some degree. For example, we may visit New York City and sit down on some random bench in order to pass the time. As we sit comfortably, our attention may begin to wander in the direction of the people who are walking by. We may start to get curious and wonder about their lives. Where are they going right now? Who are they meeting? Was it a rough day? What do they do in their private hours when no one is watching? When we venture to take a step back in our lives and watch people go about their business, we can with some degree of confidence say that we are practicing "people watching."

The problem lies in the skill itself being potentially underdeveloped and unfocused. Here is what I mean by this. Let us return back to our example of sitting on a park bench. Our attention in this example is in danger of becoming easily scattered. If our intention is to understand something about the society we live in, then without the aid of any kind of social theory, the whole endeavor can become quite difficult and unfocused.

The practice of observation needs some kind of grounding. We need to know what we are looking for when we observe other people, otherwise it may easily turn into flights of fancy.

I suggest keeping your journal with you as you do "people watching" and casually glance at the focus questions to help keep you on task. The more you practice observing with a social and theoretical structure, the easier it becomes to pick up on what you are trying to see.

When we use unobtrusive measures, we simply find a place that interests us, and this place is called a *site*. Our site is a place which we will constantly be returning to over and over again. Returning to the site will help us gather together our thoughts and research. When we pick a site, we also need to choose a time and try our best to remain faithful to the time we pick. This may be the hardest part of all.

When I teach sociology, I leave 20 minutes at the end of each class for us to go to our research sites. I am usually in charge of choosing the sites that students visit. Who goes where is usually a random process. I usually keep it this way unless a student has a strong interest in going to a particular place.

On campus, there are a number of interesting places that students can visit to help them practice these interesting research skills. For example, I send some students off to the cafeteria, to the bursar's office, to the church (if one is located on the premise), and to the library to conduct their practice in learning structured unobtrusive measures.

Sometimes out-of-the-ordinary things occur, sometimes not much happens. Other times, interesting observations are discovered by students. I am thinking of my students at a community college I teach at. They began to notice that the cafeteria was divided into two sections, one for the creative and artistic type of students and the other side was reserved for the rest of the student body and faculty. This division was maintained and regulated by this constant grouping. As they were able to ask questions and observe more deeply, they found out that the "creative and artsy" side often played imaginative games like Dungeons and Dragons, while the other side often spoke about their classes and other routine things happening in their lives.

Let me mention a few problems that might occur when we hang out in the background and watch other things unfold. For starters, a common problem is that we might become bored and nod off. This happens often when we are not engaging ourselves with the focus questions. That is why it is so crucial to keep ourselves on track by answering the questions. You can do this easily by glancing at the questions and then looking back up. Make sure you pause and take the time to write down your answers as insights come to you.

Also, some degree of presence needs to be cultivated. When "people watching," it is easy to lose our presence and so we need some technique that can help us stay present. I often recommend trying to lightly smile as we look around the area. We can also return to our breathing and casually notice it going in and out. Another way is to occasionally ask yourself silently "what social things are happening here right now?" If we can enjoy taking a step back to observe, then potentially we can be more present to what unfolds. So much for unobtrusive measures.

Participant observation is a method that is not as passive as unobtrusive measures. It is usually an active experience that becomes engaged with its research site in a different kind of way. This kind of research can be difficult at first if you are not used to looking at things sociologically.

I always recommend practicing unobtrusive measures first. You can probably divide your semester up neatly into two halves. The first half doing unobtrusive measures and the second half focusing on participant observation. I think midterm and post-midterm periods can provide a nice transition for this change in methods.

When you do participant observation, it is nice to understand a few ground rules.[ii] These few rules may seem highly obvious to you, but they need to be mentioned and constantly remembered when you undertake any kind of social research.

The first rule to remember[iii] is to try and do no harm to yourself or to other people. This rule seems obvious enough, right? When you go to your research site over a long period of time and talk with the people around you, you may begin to develop a relationship with some of them. When you record your findings in your journal, please do so with the understanding that you are to use pseudonyms for the people you interview or speak with. Pseudonyms are just alternative names you make up for the people you talk to. We never use people's real names out of respect for their privacy. If someone were to find our journal and read what is written within, it could potentially harm other people that we are writing about. Imagine a worker we interview bad mouthing the place they work for and then the manager finding their name all over our journal. We have to try and be careful when we conduct research. This rule is all about cultivating respect for other people.

A second rule to remember is to make sure you tell people that you are doing social research. You do not want to be sneaky and pretend you just happened to gain the courage that day to sit next to a group of people and start talking. If you decide to engage with other people, then please make your intentions known to them up front. I know what you might be thinking and the answer is "yes." At first, it may be a little awkward for all the parties involved, but at least it is honest. This rule is all about cultivating honesty toward other people.

After you have told people your intentions, a third rule to remember is to make sure they are okay with you jotting a few things down in your notebook. Just as it is polite to tell people what you are doing, it is also equally polite to ask their permission to jot a few things down. Of course, you will reassure them when you add that you are using pseudonyms and not their real names.

After we have an understanding of the ground rules, it is clear sailing from here. We can begin to consult the end of the chapter for structured questions that we may ask other people or think about a question that might interest us and go about trying to figure it out. A lot of the times, students that have interests come to me to ask me what to do. I may take a look at their interests and research site to help them find good ways to explore their interests best. I also tell students that it is not mandatory that they develop any kind of research question while visiting their site. It is just important at this stage to continue to develop this sociological imagination. Having observational skills that passively watch and actively engage with the social environment are two of the best ways that I know of to develop this kind of imagination.

[ii] Conley, Dalton. *You May Ask Yourself.* New York: W. W. Norton, 2013. Print.
[iii] The research rules are concisely summarized in Conley's textbook.

MY STORY DOING UNOBTRUSIVE MEASURES & PARTICIPANT OBSERVATION

When I assign the research sites to students, I frequently visit them at their sites and give them encouragement or answer any question that they may have. It is also a good way to develop friendship, a key ingredient in learning any subject matter.

One time, I went to the library and sat down with the intentions of practicing unobtrusive measures. All of a sudden an older gentleman, who was sitting right beside me began to speak to me. And a female student from my class also sat down and began to join in on the conversation. We were talking about math and how difficult it is to get people to enjoy it. I was listening attentively to the young lady and the older man.

Not long after, the librarian singled me out and told me that I needed to observe silence in this library. I immediately shut up. Meanwhile, the older man and the young lady kept conversing like nothing happened.

At the other school I teach at people are allowed to speak in the library. I thought it might be interesting to ask the librarian about this golden rule of silence. I went up to her and told her my intentions. I said I was doing social research and I was interested in why I was told to be quiet. I quickly began to notice that the older folks and women were still speaking and none of the younger men were talking at all.

The librarian spoke to me in a very gentle way. She told me the reason that she asked me to be quiet was my voice. She told me that it carried more than other peoples. She told me that usually younger men's vocals carry more loudly than others. I was a little surprised by this, but I thanked the librarian for providing me with reasons for shutting my trap.

I walked away and went to a different spot. I consciously whispered to other people and asked them if this librarian usually singles out younger men. The answers floating around the library were unanimously "yes!" I began to test whether it was just this librarian or the rule observed in general; I asked the younger ladies and men from my class to help me out with this hypothesis.

Uncovering unsaid things in the social world is one of the fruits of doing social research. We can begin to see how we structure our relationships with other people and the consequences that they can have. Do younger men's voices carry more than older folks and women? As I continue to observe what happens in the library today, I begin to see the disparity of voices being heard within that facility.

Assessment/Checklist/Questions

Exercise 1: *Instructions on how to practice unobtrusive measures*

- Choose a time and research site to visit twice a week for a semester's length of time.
- Make sure your journal and writing implement are close-at-hand.

- Record the date, time, and duration of your stay in your journal.
- Record what is happening at your site in your journal.
- Passively watch things unfold.
- Keep presence: smiling and meditation can help you with this.
- Casually glance at the focus questions and answer them.

Exercise 2: *Instructions on how to practice participant observation*

- Choose a time and research site to visit twice a week for a semester's length of time.
- Make sure your journal and writing implement are close-at-hand.
- Record the date, time, and duration of your stay in your journal.
- Record what is happening at your site in your journal.
- Actively become engaged at your research site. Do this by asking questions to people around you (general questions can be located at the end of this chapter).
- Keep presence: smiling and meditation can help you achieve this state.
- When becoming engaged with the people and the environment, try to practice being as nonjudgmental as possible. You can do this by becoming more inquisitive about the social world.
- Casually glance at the focus questions and answer them.
- Remember to observe the three general research rules: do no harm, be honest, and get permission to jot.

Focus Questions

Here are some questions you can begin to ask yourself while practicing *unobtrusive measures*. There are plenty more where this came from. And as you begin to get the hang of what you are supposed to be looking for, you can start asking questions of your own. You do not have to answer all the questions in one sitting. It might be best for you to try and answer five in one sitting. Do as many as you can gently in one sitting. Remember we are trying to structure our observations by looking for specific social things.

- What is happening around you?
  - Is the area heavily populated with people or not? What do you think that says about the area? What about the time?
  - Take a moment to look around the room: try to notice what roles other people are playing, that is, are some working while others are just hanging out?
    - What roles are they performing?
  - A question on culture: what are the people doing? Are they on the computer? The phone? Talking to each other? Reading a book? Eating? Try to be descriptive.
  - What kind of mood surrounds the area you are observing? Are people laughing? Smiling? Occupied? Standoffish?

- What are people wearing? Are some people dressed in uniform while others are not? If so, why this distinction? What does it mean?
- A question on the social categories: do you notice more of one particular gender in your area? How about race? Ethnicity? Age?
- A question on hegemony: are there advertisements around your research site? If so, what do they say? What audience do you think it is intended for? What particular social group do you think the advertisement is speaking to? What does it say about the place you are at if this kind of advertisement is there?
- Has anyone tried to talk to you or ask you for help?

Here are some questions to ask when doing *participant observation*. You will be able to tell which questions are appropriate and inappropriate in certain contexts, that is, if you are asking someone praying alone in a church if they do this for a social call, then you are probably in the wrong!

- Asking an employee: "excuse me, I am doing social research for my class."
  - Do you have a moment to talk?
  - What kind of work do you do here?
    - Can you tell me a little bit about it?
    - Can you walk me through an average day?
  - How long have you been working here for?
    - Do you enjoy it here?
    - Where were you working before you started here?
    - Was it close to this area or further away?
    - Are you from around this area? If not, where are you from?
  - What is the strangest thing you ever saw while working here?
    - If you have the time, can you please tell me about it?
- Asking a bystander: "excuse me, I am doing social research for my class."
  - Do you mind if I join you for a moment?
  - Do you come here often?
  - When did you start coming here?
  - What do you usually do while you're here?
  - Do you like the people who work here?
  - Do you like the atmosphere?
  - Is this a place where you hang out with your friends or go just to be alone?

Culture as a Way of Life

3

SUMMARY OF MAIN IDEAS: CULTURE AS MATERIAL AND NONMATERIAL

➤ Culture is a lived experience and practice that unfolds constantly in social life.

➤ Material culture is the physical things that we assign meaning and use to.

➤ Nonmaterial culture pertains to the ideas, values, and beliefs that we hold about the social world.

SUMMARY OF MAIN EXERCISE: "GO SOMEPLACE NEW"

➤ When you "go to someplace new," think of a particular place that you would like to visit. You can make this exercise your personal excuse to try something new. Once you decide on the place, then go and visit it and make sure you spend sufficient time there. If it is a restaurant, then plan on eating there! When you go to your new place, please try and pay close attention to how you're feeling and how others are receiving your visit. As always, consult the focus questions and record your experience in your journal.

Now that we have understood and practiced our sociological way of thinking and observing, we can turn our attention toward culture. Remember earlier on when we said this was one half of the sociological imagination? Well, I think it is now a good time to say a little more about what culture is and what sociologists actually mean by it. As always, our aim in doing this is to strengthen our way of thinking and living sociologically. We must never forget this aim, for the goal of sociology is to become more aware of the social world we create.

Culture is very close to us, so it is often difficult to study it. When I was doing my undergraduate work, I had a very exclusive sense of what the word culture meant. I would often think of culture as something that was foreign and exotic to my own way of living. I thought because it was so different it was therefore worth studying. This does seem reasonable enough, right? In the field of sociology, this exotic interest is unfortunately not enough.

When sociologists speak of culture, they mean everything you come to experience personally within your own life. It is often divided up into two interrelated parts. These parts are called *material* and *nonmaterial* culture.

When you think of material culture, pause momentarily to look around at all the physical materials nearby you. This is what we mean by material culture. I am pausing right now as I write this in order to look around my room. I see books, CDs, a computer, an iPod, paintings, plates, and cups. All of these things are material culture and they are filled with meaning. The culture that we continually practice helps fill this meaning up.

Let's take another moment to pause and consider what nonmaterial culture might be. It seems obvious enough to say that it is something without material. But what is *it*? As I sit down in my room thinking about what nonmaterial culture could be, I begin to notice that I am all alone in privacy. For many of us, privacy seems to be an idea that we hold dear to us.

Any ideology or value that we hold close to us would be considered an example of nonmaterial culture. I feel that the more we take a moment to think about this, the more we can begin to see some of the ideas that dwell alongside us. What do you believe in? Privacy? Equality? Helping other people? Future plans? Hard work?

Sometimes we can look at the things around us and instantly notice what we believe in and the ideologies that come along with it. For example, I may look at a book on race, class, and gender and recall the importance in my own life of trying to see the interplay of intersectionality in society. And I may even further dwell on the historical privileges and inequalities that dwell alongside the intersection of the social categories.

As I said before, culture is very close to us. Sometimes it might be hard to "see" our ideologies or even the material culture that surrounds us. We have to remember that we practice culture every day. We are so good at it that we forget to stop and take stock of it. This is part of the reason of what makes the subject difficult to study—it feels so "natural" to us.

As I say in my classes, the more "natural and obvious" something seems to be to us, the greater the chance we have at becoming thoughtless about it in our own lives. Culture becomes so natural and obvious that it becomes thoughtless of itself. It is not until we begin to develop a questioning attitude toward these seemingly "natural things" that we truly begin to notice how "unnatural" they are. This is the start of seeing culture, which is rooted in history and is a *social construction*. This is an insight worth remembering for sure.

One of the ways we can develop an understanding of culture is to step away from it. This can be done in a number of different ways. We do not need to go on an exotic vacation in order to get a glimpse at different ways of living (like I once previous thought in my undergraduate years).

There are a lot of places around our area that we have never visited before. Places that we may have passed by hundreds of times before and never gave a second thought about it. These places can provide the backdrop for the exercise of this chapter titled "go someplace new."

The exercise is exactly as it sounds. When we go someplace entirely new, we may feel slightly anxious about it. The unfamiliar can be an uncomfortable experience for us. A tagline you often now hear in sociology—and I have heard it elsewhere as well—is that *we should try and make what is routine to us somehow unusual.* This kind of attitude and practice can go a long way, and it will certainly help breathe life into what is so banal and "natural" to us.

The reason this exercise is important for understanding culture is simple. Understanding by experiencing unfamiliar social contexts can help us better understand our own familiar social contexts.

The last thing I will say concerning culture is how vastly different it is across time and space. In this chapter, my aim was to make you more aware of your own culture, and how you, in turn, practice it within your own life. But I cannot leave you to your own thoughts about culture.

I am thinking of a time when I was sitting at the kitchen table drinking my morning cup of coffee and I was looking out at the screen glass window. I happened to notice that a few cats were sitting on the deck. Suddenly they all started licking their private parts in unison the same exact way. I thought to myself, "I wonder if the cats in Bulgaria do it that same exact way?" We know that human beings do not do things exactly the same.

When thinking of humans, on the other hand, ordering a coffee or even waiting on line varies in a multiplicity of factors like context, time, and culture. There is no agreed upon way to order a coffee or how to stand in line and what to do while you stand there. Please keep this in your mind in order to protect yourself against *ethnocentrism*. Ethnocentrism is judging other cultures and their practices from your own biased point of view. If you think you know best how to order a coffee for all peoples in the world, then please think again!

MY STORY OF "GOING SOMEPLACE NEW"

When I visited the countryside of England, I went out to a number of different restaurants and pubs. Some were formal and others were not. I remember the first restaurant I ever visited there; it was a *usually* rainy day that particular day.

I decided to go ahead and try to beat the lunch rush. Keeping that in mind, I went between lunch and supper time. When I arrived there, only a handful of people were at the restaurant eating. I stood with my back against the door awkwardly. I was not sure if I should wait to be seated or just pick a booth myself. I stood in my anxiousness for about 5 minutes. I decided to pretend to look at my watch, that way I would possibly give off the impression that I was waiting for somebody else (I was actually eating alone that night).

The awkwardness became too much for me to bear, and so, I left the restaurant in haste. I still maintained my award winning performance of "waiting for a friend" role.

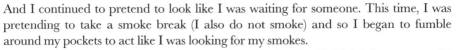

And I continued to pretend to look like I was waiting for someone. This time, I was pretending to take a smoke break (I also do not smoke) and so I began to fumble around my pockets to act like I was looking for my smokes.

I also began to develop this elaborate master plan. I still think it is a pretty solid idea! I would wait for other people to go in the restaurant and see what they did and then follow their lead. There was a window by the door which would provide me with all the visual evidence I needed. Until then, I would just hang outside in this rainy weather underneath the eaves of the restaurant and keep up the smoker façade.

Shortly after, a couple entered the restaurant. Quite a lovely couple indeed. He had a tweed jacket with a flat cap, and she had a trench coat on with a beret. I tried to show some restraint and hang back in order to not make it look obvious to fellow onlookers.

As I gazed through the window, I noticed that the couple immediately headed for a booth and put their things down. They then headed up to the register where a short conversation ensued with the cashier and a transaction was made. After they paid for their meal, they went to the bar to collect their drinks and then sat back down at their table to wait.

This is something I never witnessed before. How strange? I decided that I would not leave my post until I found out what happened next.

I remember feeling really hungry and nervous about whether the dinner crowd was going to start coming in. It was all too enticing to leave my post, but at the same time absolutely terrifying to actually move from it. The next question I roughly formulated was this: "were they supposed to go to the food and pick it up or was the food supposed to come to them?" I waited for the results, and as I did, I occasionally peaked inside the restaurant window hastily. I am really surprised no one said anything to me that day. The mixture of hunger and anxiety seemed to be unfulfilling for my disposition. Finally, after some time had passed, the lovely couple picked up their food at the register and I was floored in amazement.

Now that I witnessed a potential template, I decided to try it out for myself in a different restaurant. Come on, did you think I was going to walk back in there and finally order? No way! I was much too embarrassed to do that. So with an experimenting spirit, I figured it was time to see whether this thing works or not. My stomach was very happy to say, that at least in this particular case, it was a successful template.

While I was eating by myself, I began to think about the differences between ordering in the United States and the United Kingdom. Prior to visiting England, I never really had much initiative to leave my hometown. When we went out to eat, it was usually at a diner. I was so used to a host seating me, a waiter or waitress taking my order, giving me drinks and refills, and paying for the whole thing afterward. How spoiled did I have it there? In this little countryside in England, my whole ordering script seemed to flip on me. And in case you are wondering, yes, I did try and ask for free refills on my coffee in England and all that I received in return were some hearty English laughs!

Assessment/Checklist/Questions

Exercise: Instructions to "go someplace new"

- Take the time to plan where you want to visit.
- Try and stay there for 10–20 minutes.
- Pay attention to how you feel while there.
- Pay attention to how others are receiving you while you are there.

Focus Questions

- What is your culture?
  - Nonmaterial culture: please write a list down of five strong ideologies, values, and beliefs that you have.
  - Material culture: please write a list down of five material possessions that you find important to you. Please explain why they are important to you.
  - Is there any overlap between your material and nonmaterial culture list? Can you find any? If so, what are they?
- Exercise: "go someplace new."
  - Where did you decide to go and why?
  - What happened while you were there? If you went to a new clothing store, what was it like? Was it similar to other stores you have visited in the past? Or was it totally new? Were people helpful to you while you were there or not?
  - Did you get the feeling that you did not belong there? If so, what might that feeling have to do with culture?
  - After you depart from your unfamiliar place, please take a moment to write down how things worked there. Think about my story in England if you need an example to get you started. Here are some questions you can answer as you go along:
    - Are things done differently at this place? If so, how?
    - What did you find unusual about this place? Be specific. If you thought it was strange that they asked you for your coat, then please report that!
    - Are there similar places you have been to that remind you of this place?
      - List five things that make this an unfamiliar place.
      - List five things that you are used to seeing in places similar to this.
      - What are the similarities? What are the differences?
    - Would you ever visit this place again?

Socialization: Acting Out Social Roles

4

SUMMARY OF MAIN IDEAS: SOCIALIZATION

➤ Socialization is the ongoing process of learning how to do and internalize your experience within society.

➤ Robert Merton's role theory[i] is a specialized vocabulary designed to help us see how our social interactions with other people and ourselves spring from our identification with social categories. We are granted a status. We begin to act out that role and usually stick to a general script within that role. Other people usually help us stick and adhere to the script. Sometimes we run into problems while playing a role. In this case, we can either face role conflict or role strain. Role conflict happens when different roles that we play come into conflict. Role strain is when the role we play demands too much from us.

➤ Erving Goffman's dramaturgical theory[ii] is an attempt to view the social world as a drama unfolding on the stage of life. Our social lives are filled with drama that we act out on various stages. These dramas unfold on two particular stages: the front and the backstage, or otherwise known as the public and private spheres. Beware: the lines and stages can sometimes get blurred.

---

[i] For a further treatment of Merton and his works, please check out: Merton, Robert K. *Social Theory and Social Structure*. Illinois: The Free Press of Glencoe, 1963. Print.

[ii] A Goffman classic worth reading is: Goffman, Irving. *The Presentation of Self in Everyday Life*. New York: The Overlook Press, 1973. Print.

SUMMARY OF MAIN EXERCISES: "GET A STATUS AND PLAY A ROLE" & "BE ON THE LOOKOUT FOR BACKSTAGE ANTICS"

➤ "Get a status and play a role" is a nice little exercise that can help you get out of your usual routine. The exercise asks you to pick a character to play and act out the way you think that person would. To keep it simple, pick a place to go and visit there for a few times a week at the same exact time. Do not be afraid to dress up and create a new name for your character. At first, all of this might feel a little silly, but as you continue on, you should begin to "feel" that what you are acting is indeed real.

➤ "Be on the lookout for backstage antics" is an excellent exercise to find out where the front and backstage dramas meet and where the lines blur. Usually, you might expect to find people acting a certain way in the public eye; however, at times, you may notice that someone notably causes a "scene" in public. Goffman would say that we were lucky enough to witness someone's backstage antics. I suggest going to McDonald's or the mall. Sit someplace on the side for 20 or so minutes and be on the lookout for these dramatic "scenes" unfolding.

In this chapter, I will discuss two theories and provide two exercises to go along with them. First, I will discuss Robert Merton's role theory and then provide an exercise for you to do afterward. Later on in the chapter, I will explain Erving Goffman's dramaturgical theory and then share another sociological exercise with you that will help you see how this theory pans out in your everyday life.

Sociological Thinker

Robert Merton (1910–2003)

Major works: *Social Theory and Social Structure*

Merton was a functionalist theorist and the creator of a method known as middle range theory. To a middle range theorist, theory and practice must go hand and hand. As a functionalist, he tried to understand the function and content of institutions and roles that we play in society. He is also known for being one of the founders of the sociology of science.

First let me start off with saying a little something about the process of *socialization*. Essentially, it is the ongoing practice of learning how to do society. In sociology, we often recognize that the learning process of how to do society will never stop.

Please take a moment to consider the exercise from the last chapter. "Go someplace new" almost demands us to learn because being in a new environment brings with it unknown features that are foreign to us. As I am sure you already know from

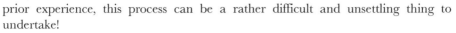

prior experience, this process can be a rather difficult and unsettling thing to undertake!

In my classes, in order to explain how the process of socialization works in everyday life, I often give the example of starting up a new job. When we are lucky enough to even get a new job, we might begin to notice that an anxious or excited feeling often accompanies it, and this might be true especially on our first day on the job. As a sociologist, I think this is because we are not only trying to learn something new—the job itself—but we are also learning and negotiating new roles and scripts with other people.

Robert Merton developed *role theory* to help create a language for this very interesting and exciting process in social life. Please allow me to briefly explain this new and exciting style of language. I hope you will find it to be as helpful and beneficial in your own life as it has been in mine.

When we get involved in new things like our job, then we begin to take on a *status*. A status helps give us a place so that other people (including ourselves) can identify and understand who we are. A good example of this would be an employee and a customer. If a person works at a restaurant, then their status is that of an employee, and even more specifically, perhaps a host, cook, waiter, or waitress. And many times employees will wear some kind of uniform that sets them apart from the customers that they serve. This is indeed no accident. When we take on a role of this kind, we need to distinguish ourselves from others, in this case, the customers. Meanwhile, the customers will notably pay for some service at this restaurant, and depending on the place or the occasion, will mostly wear nonuniforms of some sort. And if they wear a uniform, it may be of a different kind than the one the employee sports.

Now granted, this may all sound very obvious to you, and of that I am quite sure, but please consider for a moment how essential it is to know who is in what status. Have you ever been to a place where you did not know who was an employee and who was a customer? Not having this kind of information can be a very frustrating and unpleasant experience.

Merton noted that once we have our status and it is known to all parties involved, then we usually begin to play out a *role*. A role is simply a set of expectations that all of us who are involved have about how to play the role correctly. If we are an employee at a restaurant, we may ask people if they need help, keep ourselves busy working, and smile a lot as we take customer orders. If we did all this sequentially, then we might be said to be living up to the expectations of our role and doing a good job at work. If we, on the other hand, decided to go outside to meditate and help walk other people's dogs, then we could be said to be not performing the "employee working at a restaurant" role adequately enough. And this could cause us to lose our job or even be shunned by our fellow workers as a complete "weirdo." Can you now see that obtaining a status and learning how to play out a role is indeed a process of socialization?

Merton was also interested in what it takes to make certain roles function smoothly and also how they relate to different roles that we might have. He observed (probably through his own life experience) that sometimes one role we play may demand too much from us. When our role demands too much from us, then we experience what he called *role strain*. As students, we can relate to this concept very much. My students complain that some of their Professors act like their course is the only course anyone takes and they assign excessive amounts of work. These students may be taking five classes with five different professors and each Professor may be handing out an unreasonable amount of work during that semester. Merton would say that a student being pulled in five different directions would definitely experience role strain. Their role as a student and the expectation that surrounds them is literally asking too much.

Merton was also interested in how one role might influence other roles that we are involved in. When we begin to experience numerous difficulties at school, with our families and friends, and at a similar time, then we can be said to be in *role conflict*. Imagine that during finals week, your work keeps piling up (student role) and you are having problems with your mom and dad (son/daughter role) and some of your friends want you to forget your schoolwork and go out with them for some drinks (friendship role). This might sound like an everyday affair for many of us, but Merton just gave us a special language to name the process: role conflict.

We all play different roles and they all clash with one another. So what? What can *we* do about it? Merton would say that once we become aware and identify the roles that we play, and the expectations that surround each one, we can then begin the process of transforming them.

Right now as I write this particular sentence, I am thinking of a woman in one of my classes; she was a very kind and endearing sort of person. She felt like she was trapped in a certain role that she was playing. Luckily for us, she was brave enough to speak about it in front of the whole class. She pointed out that whenever she spoke to her mom one-on-one, she usually "read" from the hateful script.

When we play a role and repeatedly return to a similar context, we tend to read familiar lines from the same script. Have you ever noticed yourself having the same fights over and over again with someone? Well, once we become aware that this is the script that we usually read from, then we can choose not to read from it and pick another one. It sounds easy, right? This is one of those cases where the adage "easier said than done" applies. I think this is because other actors and actresses on the stage of life will often push us back into our old ways, roles, and scripts. We have to be careful and aware in our daily lives, so that we avoid entering into that hateful script again. Believe me, it can be a very liberating process when you become aware of your statuses, roles, and scripts. As soon as you recognize the loop, you can (with much effort) hop out of it.

In the first exercise of this chapter, we are going to consciously take on a new status and play out the role that goes along with it. This can be done in a few different ways, and please feel free to be creative with it—I definitely encourage it!

The exercise is called "get a status and play a role." I used to call this exercise by its other moniker "early Halloween" because we dressed up as someone that we are normally not. However, I had to change the name when one student took it literal and dressed up in her Halloween garb. It was a humorous situation indeed, but it nearly scared another class to death when she randomly walked into their classroom.

Once we pick a character and dress up, we can then assume the role of that character or at least what we think that role might be. It can be very insightful and liberating to act out a different role in your life. You are so used to playing only yourself! Personally, I decided to visit a coffee shop twice a week where I dressed up in a nice suit. There I drank a cup of coffee and read the newspaper like a pro. I really got into the role and I was constantly checking my watch and acting like I was a very busy and important person. I sipped my coffee with my pinky finger extended and shook my paper from time to time and always looked very serious and informed. People were very polite to me. I put on airs about myself in a way I normally would not, and everything I did was negotiated by me as my "performing business person" script.

Speaking about playing a role, another closely related theory is Erving Goffman's *dramaturgical theory*. A lot of my students love this theory because they feel it explains so much about how our society works.

Sociological Thinker

Erving Goffman (1922–1982)

Major works: *The Presentation of Self in Everyday Life*, *Strategic Interaction*, and *Interaction Ritual*

Goffman was an American sociologist who contributed a great deal to the theory of symbolic interactionism. He took interest in our everyday social interactions; he called this impression management. For him, we all seemed to act out our dramas on various stages of life.

Keeping along with the social fact that we all seem to play roles in society, we must also acknowledge that we act out these dramatic roles to other people and to ourselves. In Goffman's language, we can always locate ourselves somewhere on the social stage of life. What is essential to our enterprise is to locate which stage we are actually on. Luckily, it will not be too difficult for us, since there are only two stages in his theory: *front stage* and *backstage*.

Front stage is the performance we put on for other people in our impression management world. It usually happens, and not always, in a public setting. These front stage performances are our signature roles that most people happen to know us by. When we hang out with our friends we perform on the "friend stage." When we go to class we are acting on the "classroom stage." Social life is seemingly a theatrical performance. Can you think about what you are usually like on these two stages? Are they similar or different?

Backstage is a place that is private and off limits to most people in our lives. We might never wish for our teacher to see our backstage antics. Imagine if we all knew what happened on each other's backstages? When I think of backstage antics, I always think of the nice sweet and kind person who we all cherish as being the very definition of kind, but meanwhile in their private lives they are a totally angry and obnoxious human being. Goffman would tell me that I am usually seeing that person's front stage performance. It is when I gain access to view that angry and obnoxious performance that I earn a backstage pass.

Sometimes our backstage performance can spill over into our front stage and the people who have never seen us perform in this role might be startled. Think about a time when you saw someone patiently waiting and then suddenly their patience wore off—what happened next? Goffman would say that you were lucky enough to witness a private backstage performance.

A nice little exercise that might help you witness some of these little backstage moments is to hang around in a public place (a mall is usually good for this). I call it "be on the lookout for backstage antics." Simply sit around and wait to see if a backstage episode happens. I have found that hanging out in the parking lot or on a bench can be good waiting areas for backstage performances. Frustrated families taking their children out to dinner usually merits a backstage performance. Just simply wait awhile and see if you can see something. If nothing comes, just think of a time when you happened to witness something that was particularly backstage worthy.

Assessment/Checklist/Questions

Exercise 1: Instructions to "get a status and play a role"

- Take some time to think about what character you want to act out.
- Find the costume that matches the character.
- Frequent the same place at the same time for 20 minutes or so.
- Try to keep yourself in character.

Exercise 2: Instructions to "be on the lookout for backstage antics"

- Visit a place that you feel is perfect for witnessing "backstage" moments, that is, a mall, a grocery store, McDonald's, or some other fast food joint.
- Seat yourself out of the way and be attentive to what is happening around you.
- Try and name which stage you are seeing as you see it—is it front or backstage?
- If no backstage antics occur, then consider a time when you did see something that was backstage worthy.

Focus Questions

- Write a list down of major events in your life's trajectory and the roles that you played.
  - How did you transition from one role to the next?
  - Was that role transition difficult for you?
- Please list five statuses you have.
  - How do you play each role? Describe a typical script you might use while playing that role, that is, how do you act out "friend role" or "relationship role?"
  - Do you think that certain roles you play demand too much from you? If so, why do you think that is? If not, explain how the role fits just right for you.
  - Do multiple roles ever come into conflict in your life? If so, which roles are conflicting?

- What does your personal backstage look like? What does your front stage look like?
  - Please describe five characteristics of how you perform on each of these stages. Are they similar? Or different?
- Exercise 1: Get a status and play the role.
  - What character did you decide to play?
  - Where did you decide to go?
  - Why was this a good spot for your character to perform?
  - Did you manage to stay in character? If not, was it difficult trying to play a different role in public?
  - How did you feel playing a new role? How does this role compare to your own personal everyday role? Is there any overlap between these roles? Is there any difference between these roles?
  - How do you think other people received your character? Was this a space that embraced this type of character? Or was it a space that did not embrace your character? If not, why do you think this place was unwelcoming to your character? What kind of places do you tend to find this character dwelling at?
- Exercise 2: "Be on the lookout for backstage antics."
  - Where did you decide to go?
  - What was it like to experience someone else's backstage antics?
  - What did they do that qualifies as a backstage antic?
  - After you saw them perform live on the backstage, did it change your perspective on this person? Why? Or why not?
  - Do you think that everyone has a backstage and a front stage? Why or why not?

Basic Social Groups 5

SUMMARY OF MAIN IDEAS

➤ Sociation[i] is a basic concept for social interaction. It looks at whether social interaction holds us together or tears us apart. Whatever holds us together is called association, while whatever tears us apart is called dissociation.

➤ A dyad is a group of two people, while a triad[ii] is a group of three people.

➤ The "looking glass self"[iii] is a concept developed by Charles Horton Cooley, and it basically states that we adjust who we are based upon what we think other people think about us.

➤ Primary groups and secondary groups[iv] is another idea developed by Charles Horton Cooley. It mainly deals with the quality of group relationships. Primary groups are relationships that may last a lifetime, that is, our families and our closest friends. Secondary groups are relationships centered on some kind of purpose, and therefore people often come and go as they please. These groups are a means to an end. When thinking about secondary groups, think about your college class. Although a class loses many or all of its students at the end of each semester, it also gains many more during the following semester. This secondary group thrives even when all of its people leave.

---

[i] Check out this work for more on Simmel's sociation and social forms: Wolff, Kurt H. *The Sociology of Georg Simmel*. London: The Free Press, 1950. Print.

[ii] The treatment of these concepts is also to be found within the above-mentioned work.

[iii] If you are interested further in looking into this notion, please see: Cooley, C. H. *Human Nature and the Social Order*. New York: Scribner's, 1922. Print.

[iv] Cooley, C. H. *Social Organization: A Study of the Larger Mind*. New York: Scribner's, 1909. Print.

SUMMARY OF MAIN EXERCISES

➤ "Please give up the seat, dyad" is a simple but intimidating exercise to perform. Visit a place alone where two or three strangers are seated (usually a café or lunch table will do just fine) and ask them to give up their seats for you. Make sure to ask them nicely. Do not give a reason for why you are asking this of them. And after asking them to give up their seats, please take a minute or so to wait for their response.

➤ "Please give our triad your seat" is quite a different experience than the previous exercise. Now ask some friends of yours to join you (one or two other people will do) and ask someone sitting solitary for their seat. Remember to ask them nicely. Also, give no reasons for your seemingly random request. Observe what happens.

We cannot get very far with doing any kind of sociology unless we look at group relations and social interactions. Remember from the last chapter that social interactions help create the roles that we play and perform in society. These social interactions depend on us socializing both verbally and nonverbally with other people.

We are lucky that one sociological thinker in particular happened to occupy himself with attempting to understand group interactions. His name was Georg Simmel, and he helped create a language that can aid us in understanding what we are observing when we look at social groups.

Sociological Thinker

Georg Simmel (1858–1918)

Major works: *On Individuality and Social Forms*, *The Philosophy of Money*, and *The Sociology of Georg Simmel*

Simmel is considered one of the four European founders of Sociology, alongside Max Weber, Emile Durkheim, and Karl Marx. His approach is notable compared to those other sociological thinkers. Simmel opted to study society at a micro level. By keeping his focus grounded in the everyday interactions, he keenly observed different types of characters that happen to appear in our own everyday lives.

We build our lives around social groups—they are so fundamental to us. All groups are held together by something Simmel called *sociation*. What is sociation though? Sociation is "that thing" that brings us together mutually or pulls us apart. If it brings us together, then it is called *associative*. If it pulls us apart, it is called *dissociative*. Sociation acts as a bridge between individuals and other people and it varies in context. When we walk back and forth across the bridge, it is called social interaction. Please take a look at this little illustration to get a picture of what I mean by all this:

Sociation of a social group: {self ← social interaction → other}

Without social interaction, we cannot have society, because society consists of various kinds of social groups interacting with one other. As we go about our lives, each of us practices being involved in various groups. It is all really elementary. When you go to class, you may see some of your friends and choose to sit by them. You may not talk to your friends while the teacher is lecturing, but you are still participating in the function of sociation. Since who you are as a person is essentially occupied with social groups, I would like to take a moment to mention a sociologist, who I think can help us explain this relationship more clearly.

Charles Horton Cooley helps us see that whoever we think we are often comes from what other people think about us. This is something that he called the *looking glass self*.

Sociological Thinker

Charles Horton Cooley (1864–1929)

Major works: *Human Nature and the Social Order* and *Social Organization*

Cooley was an American sociologist who was well known for his concept of *looking glass self*, which basically stated that we adjust who we are based on what others think about us. Cooley focused intimately on the social concept of the self and the quality of the group it aligns itself with.

Imagine a world in which you are surrounded by nothing but mirrors. Cooley would argue that this is the normal world in which we all usually find ourselves in, except instead of the mirrors, it is other people who reflect back to us. These people can act as mirrors to us in many different ways. Imagine spitting on the ground and receiving a dirty look by someone who passes by you. Their dirty look might be enough to prevent you in the future from spitting near other people again.

The way people look at us can be a very powerful and influential thing. Have you ever sat in your car or somewhere in public and thought that you were alone? Well, what happened when you were about to do something that you knew was not a very normative thing to do like fixing your underwear or picking your nose? Did you look around and see if other people might be watching you or did you just go for it? If you did look around for other people, then you can begin to understand something essential about what the looking glass self is and how it affects our lives.

Sometimes it is exhausting to be out in public with constant eyes watching us. We may finally feel a sense of relief when we get home and start doing some of the non-normative things we enjoy like passing some gas, picking our noses, and taking our pants off. Is this the stuff that backstage performances are made of?

Now that we have talked a little bit about sociation, social interaction, and the looking glass self, let us now move on to talk about specific types of groups and what they consist of. A dyad group is obviously a form of sociation. Let us take a moment to think about some dyad relationships that we might have formed within our own lives. Remember that dyad is a group of two people. Is this person you are thinking of a friend of yours? Perhaps a significant other? How about just a casual acquaintance that you normally say "hello" to each morning as you grab your coffee from the café? If they are a friend of yours, then this can mean many things for you.

I once had a friend of mine tell me that two of his closest friends no longer speak to each other anymore. This, of course, was very sad news for me to hear, and I wondered why they no longer spoke. My friend agreed and he told me that they were very close at one point and happened to be the best of friends. He told me the reason was that once they graduated college and moved away from each other, they simply lost contact. Has something like this ever happened to you? When we begin to think about this happening in our own lives, we begin to notice how delicate dyad relationships can really be. And it also says something about what a dyad group actually is like. This group is very delicate because if one of the members decides to walk away, then the whole thing is finished.

Let us not specifically focus on the potential negative factors of a dyad group. Besides being delicate, a dyad group also has the quality of being the most intimate group that we can have within our lives. What I mean by this might sound obvious to you, but let us just dwell on it for a moment or two. Think about a party you might have attended recently. What happened when all the people left and you were just left alone with another friend or a significant other? Did you talk to them differently? Have you ever had a significant other tell you that you act differently in front of a group of people than when you are alone together?

Group dynamics can be a very fascinating thing to study. The key thing is to start thinking this sort of way about your own life as it currently unfolds. Are you alone as you read this book? Are you sitting down on a park bench with a few friends as you peruse these pages? How about at home with your family? Or perhaps your roommate is moving around frantically and annoying your solitude? After you finish reading this chapter or page, are you going to go out and meet another friend or perhaps maybe a couple? We should try and see if we can develop a way of thinking sociologically about these types of events in our lives.

Now what happens when we add one more person to a dyad group? We get a *triad*! A triad is a social group of three people. When we have three people in our group, then the dynamic of the group changes dramatically and it becomes more complex. When we talked about what a triad is in my class, a student told me that he had a somewhat sad example that related to the subject. He told us that he once had three wonderful friends. Two of them were guys and one was a girl. Well, two of the friends happened to be dating at the time, and when it did not work out between the two of them, the other two shortly started up a relationship together. As it happens to turn out, this event was enough to upset the group's harmony, and part of the group, namely the ex-boyfriend, then decided to leave the group for good. Can you immediately notice something different from the dyad dynamic? Even though one member of the group walked away, the group seemed to continue on. In fact, the student told me that they are still dating and going strong, but the former member of the triad was never able to make amends with either one of them. Maybe that dyad will be able to find another "third wheel" to mend their broken triad?

Sometimes a triad can form something like a "third wheel." Maybe you might know something about "third wheels" yourself and how they play out in society. I am thinking of the film *Shaun of the Dead*,[v] where one of the main characters plays an excellently annoying "third wheel" to the other two who are in a relationship. Third wheels can be awkward for us and can often put us in role conflict—remember that term from the last chapter, right? Can you think of any example of different types of triads that you have been in? Have you ever starred in the role as the infamous "third wheel?" If so, what was that group dynamic like? Did you act differently together as a triad than when you hung out with one of them in a dyad group?

Two group exercises that we can try out for ourselves in order to study group dynamics involve us asking politely for other people's chairs. By yourself, go up to a triad group sitting at a table and nicely ask all of them for their seats. And please see what happens.

After you try this out for yourself and write down your results, try finding two other people and form a triad of your own. Afterward, go to another table where one person is sitting alone and nicely ask them for their seat. If in either case someone lets you take their table and seat, you can immediately let them know that it was just a little social experiment and thank them for their time. And if you feel bad about the whole ordeal, you can buy them a cup of coffee and explain how crazy your teacher is for assigning you these sociological exercises.

And what about backstage behavior? Can we in some way tie group thinking into Goffman's dramaturgical theory? Remember what you read earlier on in this chapter. When you are alone with another person, do you perform and act differently than you would normally to other people? There are certain sociologists who would say that we perform roles differently depending on the group size and the quality of the group we are in. As I write this sentence, I am reminded about Cooley's *primary* and *secondary groups*.

Cooley's primary groups, in particular, deal with quality relationships that we have that may last a lifetime. When he talks about primary groups, he is thinking about our families, friends, significant others, and relatives. People that we happen to love and feel deep affection for and are there for us throughout our lives. As may be expected, these groups of people tend to play a crucial role in our lives. They might even be the most consistent relationships that we have in life, even though they might not be the most stable or amiable.

There is something about these groups of people that lasts and goes beyond many of our social encounters. I think we may all agree that when we are ordering a coffee at a café and we speak to the cashier, the quality of that relationship might end if they stop working there or stop serving us coffee. The coffee might be the only means that holds our little group together as we come to the café every day for our caffeine fix. This is definitely not a primary group, agreed?

---

[v] I reference the movie to show the often humorous and ridiculous "third wheel" situation. If you lack any example of your own, then please watch this film!

In primary groups, it is more than just the coffee that holds us together. These groups are an end in themselves. Please allow me to provide a great example of this for you. What if we lost our job and had nowhere to go? Who would take us in? What if our family took us back in and we did not even have to pay them anything at all? Our family may be one such group that does this sort of thing in society. And remember that in society usually everything comes with a price!

Assessment/Checklist/Questions

Exercise 1: Instructions for the exercise "please give up the seat, dyad"

- Go to a public place where there are tables, that is, a library, café, etc.
- Find a dyad/triad that is sitting down together.
- By yourself, ask them nicely if you can please have the whole table for yourself.
- Do not explain yourself.
- Even if they emphatically say "no!" continue to stand there for one or two extra minutes and wait.
- If they are about to leave their table, then please say it was a social experiment and afterward depart.

Exercise 2: Instructions for the exercise "please give our triad your seat"

- Ask a friend or two to join you for this venture.
- Go to a public place with tables.
- Find a person sitting alone.
- With your dyad/triad as unintimidating as possible, ask them for their seat.
- Do not explain yourself.
- Even if they emphatically say "no!" continue to stand there for one or two extra minutes and wait.
- If they are about to give up their seat, then please let them know that it was a social experiment and afterward depart.

Focus Questions

- Please take a few moments to list some of your primary groups.
- Describe a dyad group you have been a part of—what was it like? Think about that same person, but add one extra person. Does the dynamic change between you and this person? If so, how? And in what way?
- Does your dyad example act differently in public than when in private? If so, what is different and why?
- Exercise 1: "Please give up the seat, dyad."
  - Did you experience different results with each of these experiments? If so, what were they?

○ What was the experience like standing alone and asking a dyad/triad group for their seats?

○ Did the dyad/triad group quickly move out of your way or did they just stay put?

- Exercise 2: "Please give our triad your seat."

  ○ What was the experience like when you were a dyad/triad asking one person for their seat?

  ○ Did that one person move immediately when your group asked for their seat?

Social Control and Deviance

6

SUMMARY OF MAIN IDEAS

➤ Deviance is breaking any norm whether formal or informal.

➤ Social control is the regulation of these formal or informal norms that are upheld by most people in various contexts.

➤ Labeling theory[i] is assigning a status and role to another person (as well as oneself) and having that person over time internalize it.

➤ Primary and secondary deviance[ii] is the process by which labeling theory unfolds. Primary deviance is really the first deviant action the actor performs. Other people make the deviant action known through social control. Secondary deviance is every similar instance that follows after primary deviance.

SUMMARY OF MAIN EXERCISES

➤ "Go someplace you do not belong" is a sociological exercise that asks you to visit a place where you feel like you do not belong. Some examples include visiting a bar for an underage student, going to a daycare center while sporting a moustache, all the way to hanging out at your local police station for no reason at all. It can also be as simple as a man visiting the women's lingerie section or a woman visiting a cigar shop filled with old-timer's.

➤ "Stare someone down when they do the 'right' thing" is a fun little exercise that involves tiny attempts on our part to shift the norms. You are

[i] Becker, H. S. *Outsiders: Studies in the Sociology of Deviance.* New York: The Free Press, 1963. Print.
[ii] Lemert, Edwin. *Human Deviance, Social Problems and Social Control.* Englewood Cliffs, NJ: Prentice-Hall, 1967. Print.

deliberately asked to give people dirty looks when they do something that is normatively correct in that context. An example would be giving someone a mean look as they hold the door for you. You could also look at someone as if they have five heads when they attempt to shake your hand or say "hello" to you. Bring your friends along and have them try this exercise with you. There certainly is power in numbers.

Have you ever heard that we are influenced by what other people think about us? Sounds a little bit like Cooley's "looking glass self," right? Well, instead of looking at who we are as a self, we are now going to turn our attention specifically to how other people influence our actions and behaviors. I am thinking mainly about what is considered deviant in our society. *Deviance* is an action (physical/mental) of people that is deemed wrong; it is essentially violating the informal and formal norms of society.

Let us narrow it down a bit and think about some of the informal things that are deviant in society. Try and think about some situations that you have been in, which you thought were deviant but really did not merit any serious jail time. Please take a moment to write down at least five informal deviant situations that you have been in during the course of your life. If you are having trouble starting your list, look below at some of my examples.

How about when you held up the line at the grocery store? If you have not done this before, then the next time you go to the grocery store, please try and notice how other people muscle you out of the way. When you are about to enter your pin number into the machine, the person right behind you quickly begins to inch into your space. Notice how the cashier even starts to ring up this next person immediately, as you try and scramble to put your money away and bag up your groceries as quickly as you can. The whole experience of rushing people is stressful, right? Please try and notice these things for yourself as they exactly happen in your life. Maybe you were that person who bullied the customer into rushing their bagging job? I wonder what this says about our society and how we socially interact with each other in a public setting.

Please allow me to contrast this American supermarket etiquette with the English experience of shopping for groceries. When I was studying over in England, I noticed that customers and cashiers silently waited until the transaction was entirely finished. I mean *entirely* finished. That includes the time it took for me to put my money away in my wallet and coin purse, as well as, the time it took for me to bag up my groceries! I was amazed with this subtle difference! I was almost stressed out that no one on the queue was stressed out.

I remember this one time when I was standing in the queue (the line) waiting to be served, a gentleman cut in front of me and the cashier saw him do it (by the way, the queue was particularly long that day); anyways, the cashier admonished the gentleman and told him to go to the back of the queue or he would not get served that day. Wow! The queue has a power of its own over there.

As I mentioned before, deviance can be a very subtle matter, but please do try and notice how it influences your own behavior in these situations. Do you rush to put your money in your wallet? Do you turn on your "quick bagging action" skills in order to immediately get your groceries out of the way for the next person in line? Our way of acting in society is being highly shaped by the other people that we encounter (hint: "looking glass self").

Deviance can be found all around us, and so the regulation of it by us is something that we in sociology call *social control*.[iii] Social control is exactly how it sounds. It is the opposite of breaking norms, and so, it generally means following the rules. Emile Durkheim had some pretty insightful things to say about what social control is. Durkheim noticed that most of us seem to follow the rules pretty well. In order for us to really do this successfully, we need rule-breakers to help us maintain these rules and give meaning to them. When I tell students that deviance is seen as something integral in society, it comes as somewhat of a shock to them. After a while of studying deviance within our own lives, we might begin to see the utility of what this insight might mean.

Sociological Thinker

Emile Durkheim (1858–1917)

Major works: *Suicide, Division of Labor in Society,* and *The Rules of Sociological Method*
Durkheim was a famous French sociologist. He is considered one of the four European founders of the discipline of sociology. He was the first recognized academic sociologist and he was partly responsible for making sociology into a legitimate academic field of study.

But what does this mean for us? This major insight of Durkheim's roughly means that we need deviant people in order for society to function at all. It might come as no surprise to you that Durkheim was a *functionalist*. All you need to know about functionalism right now is that it is a theory that attempts to view the function of each part of society. A functionalist searches for a certain part of society and attempts to view how it functions and relates to the whole. If you happened to ask a functionalist what the function of deviance is in society, then they might respond by telling you that rule-breakers first of all help us create and enforce the rules. Secondly, they might tell you that all societies need deviant people to transgress the limits of society, so that we, the rule-followers, might then be able to know what the limits are and build our laws around that. Does that make sense? Thanks to Durkheim's insight, we now know that to some extent, we need deviant people to help us figure out what normative behavior really is.

But what about those formal and informal acts of deviance? Who is it that really creates deviance? Is it simply the person who commits deviant acts, namely, the

---

[iii] Take a gander at Emile Durkheim's work on Suicide to get a fuller treatment of social control. Durkheim, Emile. *Suicide: A Study in Sociology.* New York: The Free Press, 1951. Print.

rule-breaker? Maybe Durkheim would say that is their function, right? But let us not stop here, though. One good insight deserves another. Let us see if we cannot push a little further.

I want to ask for help from two sociological thinkers and one in particular. The first is an American sociologist named Howard S. Becker and the other an Austrian-American named Frank Tannenbaum.[iv] For the remainder of this chapter, however, we will spend our time focusing specifically on what Becker has to say.

Sociological Thinker

Howard S. Becker (1928–)

Major works: *Outsiders: Studies in the Sociology of Deviance*
    Becker is an important American sociologist who studies deviance. He is known for his contributions to labeling theory, a move that attempts to see more than just the deviant person as being involved in the process of labeling.

In the last chapter, we spoke a little bit about the power of group dynamics. If you did your homework of rallying together a dyad or triad and asking a solitary for their seat, then you know exactly what I am talking about here. If you have not done so, then please return to Chapter 5 and conduct the social experiment for yourself before going on any further. It is important that we experience these things for ourselves with awareness.

So there is certainly power in groups. The old adage "power in numbers" seems to ring especially true in this case. I would also like to remind you that there is power in status. Remember Merton's role theory, right? As soon as we gain any kind of status, other people begin to help us act out the role and read from the appropriate script. Believe me, people will let you know what to do in certain situations—do not worry!

A classic thought experiment might bring all this out a little more clearly for us. Please think for a moment about a teacher disciplining a child in the classroom. I think a sociologist named Edwin Lemert can help us fill in the blanks here. Once our child commits the first act of breaking the classroom rules, he calls it *primary deviance*. And the teacher thereby punishes the child to let them know that it is a deviant behavior and other students may learn from this situation. So far, nothing looks too drastic, right? It seems like standard procedure. But what if the child breaks the same rule over and over again? Lemert would call these subsequent acts of the child *secondary deviance*.

The gist of all this is that if a child gets in trouble a few times, the teacher might begin to label the child as a "bad student" or a "troublemaker" or both. Once a student receives a negative label by a person in a position of power, then they are granted to act out the socializing trio of status, role, and script. And this dynamic

[iv] An important name, but I do not plan to give fuller treatment to his contributions here. Please check out: Tannenbaum, F. *Crime and Community*. London and New York: Columbia University Press, 1938. Print.

between student and teacher can begin to become somewhat normal and even comfortable for the classroom. "Here we go again, 'teach' and 'Buford' are having it out once again. Buford is probably going to get yelled at and sent to the office again!" And the class can have a humorous laugh at the expense of it all. Over a period of time, however, the student—Buford in this case—may begin to feel as if this is what and how they really are. Buford might start to believe that this dance is what he is destined to do.

Deviance and social control hang together like peanut butter and jelly. The second major insight of this chapter is to show that while society needs deviant people, it is really the nondeviant people that create them. This statement is really the special insight of labeling theory. It can help us see that our actions of defining what is normal ultimately affects and creates the deviance around us. I think that this special insight brings with it a responsibility. We really have to be more careful in our actions and thoughts toward other people! Can you begin to see the importance of developing a sociological imagination and trying to live it out?

In this chapter, I would like to put forward two exercises we can use in order to see deviance and social control. In order to help us see deviance in an informal way, we can "go someplace where we do not belong." This is similar to "go someplace you've never gone before," but slightly different. For that exercise, you are examining your own culture while being in a unique context. This social exercise asks you to really consider someplace you think you do not belong and go and frequent it. When you go please notice the mood of the place, the looks, and the interactions you may face while you are there.

One courageous student of mine took this exercise very serious and went to visit a daycare center. He walked into the building, an 18-year-old male with no children of his own, and just strolled around the premises. While he was there, a barrage of questions were thrown in his direction and he was soon escorted off the premises. Later on, he said that as soon as he was confronted by the workers, he began to feel guilty for even showing up there! He mentioned that the workers immediately started making him feel like he was the one who was in the wrong. And this was even after they raised their voices at him and spoke to him like he was a rotten person. Imagine this kind of feeling extended across space and time in our own lives. This first exercise is all about putting yourself in a situation that can be viewed as deviant.

While in the first exercise we are looking and becoming aware of how others see us, in our second exercise, we are the ones who get to dish out the dirty looks to other people and notice how other people take them. I think it is good to feel what it is like to be on both sides of the fence, so that it can help us build compassion. I call this exercise "stare people down when they do the 'right' thing." A lot of students ask me how to do this exercise. It is really easy if you take the time to think about normal everyday things that we all might do in our social lives. When you see them playing out before your eyes, then you just give some bewildering look to that person. You can bring a couple of friends with you to help you practice social control. When someone holds the door for you, you can cast a dirty glance in their direction. When someone tries to shake your hand, you can look at them like they have lost all their marbles. When someone asks you "how are you?" you can then say "ew!"

Try and find ways of letting people know that the "normal" way of doing things is wrong. This is a conscious exercise in social control. Although you will not have the power in numbers to change some of these so-called normal things permanently, it will certainly leave the other person scratching their heads and asking themselves if it was indeed them who did something wrong.

MY STORY OF "GOING SOMEPLACE I DID NOT BELONG"

When I was thinking about where I do not belong in society, I instantly thought of going to another classroom while a class was in session. I thought to myself "well, I am a teacher, right? Let me see if I get a 'free teacher pass' to go to any class I desire."

After convincing myself that this was an experiment for the sake of sociology, and after getting a little courage to place myself in such an awkward situation, I decided to walk into another classroom and take a seat where I could find one.

Immediately, I felt all the eyes of the room on me (including the teacher's authoritative eyes). I saw some of my students in that class bewildered that I was even there. I guess that their bewilderment settled down when they realized I was just doing the homework assignment! Now, mind you, the class was not in some big lecture hall that seats hundreds of people, it was just held in a small classroom that fills up approximately 25 students. The semester was already well underway and there could be no mistaking who was and was not in that class. Everyone seemed to be performing Goffman's normative *civil inattention*, which simply means, they were not interacting directly with each other, but knew who was supposed to be there and who was not.

I managed to stay in the class for a while and I was starting to feel like I was "accepted." I started to drop my tense shoulders. Soon after I did this action, the teacher turned toward my direction and asked me if he could help me. The room was filled with silence and now it was acceptable for all the eyes in the room to face my direction. Wow, the power of all those disapproving eyes, it was intense! All those eyes looking at me could not mistake what was "wrong" with that picture in the room. Deviance is like looking at a cheesy landscape painting and suddenly splattering pink all over the bottom corner: it obviously sticks out! I told the teacher that I heard this lovely lecture on psychology from across the hall and decided to join in and listen to it. I told the teacher that I fancied knowledge of self above all and hoped that I could gain some wisdom from this encounter. The teacher responded boldly, "That is all fine and well, but I am going to have to ask you to leave now!"

A sense of shame came over me and I am pretty sure my face turned red. I got up and all the eyes followed me to my exit. After I left so did the tension. I sat down and recorded how strange it feels to be within the grips of a powerful status like a teacher. I also thought how the students maintained the normality of the class by constantly "eyeing me down."

Another time, I decided to do the other exercise "stare people down when they do the 'right' thing." Someone was introducing themselves to me in the hallway.

They put out their right hand as if they wanted me to shake it. I gave them a disapproving look and told that person "what's the matter with you?" Their face turned red and they apologized to me immediately. Afterward, I went down to the cafeteria to purchase a coffee. I expected the cashier to look me in the eye (and they did) and I gave them a mean look and said "shame on you." I stood there for an additional 30 seconds to make the whole thing more uncomfortable for the two of us. They said "I am really sorry, did I short change you?" And they scrambled to find out what happened. How weird is it to make people feel wrong about their actions?

Assessment/Checklist/Questions

Exercise 1: *Instructions to "go someplace you do not belong"*

- Take some time to think about a place you might feel unwelcomed at. Please make sure that it is a safe place.
- Visit this place.
- Notice the mood of the place.
- Notice how people receive you.
- Walk around for a little while to experience the atmosphere of the place and then leave.

Exercise 2: *Instructions to "stare people down when they do the 'right' thing"*

- Think of times and instances throughout the day when you may encounter some kind of normative behavior.
- Focus on making these interactions seem like the other person is wrong.
- You may do this by giving a dirty look, making some kind of audible sound like a sigh, or be intentionally vague with an expression like my example of saying "shame on you."
- Try and act confident when rebuking others.
- Try to record five instances of this.
- Notice the response of the other person.
- Record each experience afterward.
- You may apologize to them afterward!

Focus Questions

- Please write down five or so informal norms that you encounter throughout your daily life.
- Exercise 1: "Go someplace you do not belong."
  - Did you feel you were being deviant by going to this place? Did you feel "wrong" for going there? If so, why do you think that is?

○ How did other people's looks at this place make you feel?

○ Do you think you were treated fairly while you were there? Or do you think you were deliberately singled out? If not, why do you think that was?

● Exercise 2: "Stare people down when they do the 'right' thing."

○ What were some of the responses you received while doing this exercise?

○ Did the person throw a dirty look right back at you? If so, how did it make you feel?

○ Did you do this exercise by yourself or with other people?

■ If you did it by yourself, what kind of response did you receive from the other person or persons?

■ If you did it with other people, how many people were with you? Was your group larger than the group you gave the look to? Did you group approach one person? Please clarify what happened as you let people know they were doing the wrong thing.

Practice Poverty to Grasp Social Stratification

7

SUMMARY OF MAIN IDEAS

➤ Social stratification is the hierarchical ranking and valuing of people based on a multiplicity of factors found in the social categories.

➤ Strain theory is a theory developed by Robert Merton.[i] Merton notices that deviance occurs because society tells us what we should have and does not give us equal opportunities to procure it.

➤ Stigmatization is a negative label that greatly affects the way other people look at you and treat you and it also affects how you feel about yourself.

➤ Surveys are a series of questions intended to be filled out by groups of people. It is a great way to collect a mass amount of information and save some time while doing it. After collecting enough information, a sociologist proceeds to try and "read" and analyze the data in order to find out certain things about society.

➤ Master status is a status that surpasses all your other statuses. Essentially, it becomes the status that you are patently known by.

SUMMARY OF MAIN EXERCISES

➤ "Practice poverty" is an exercise we perform for many reasons. The Stoic philosophers[ii] used it to help them combat the fear of losing everything and also to cultivate gratitude for what they had. As sociologists, we are

---

[i] Please see this work for fuller treatment: Merton, Robert K. *Social Theory and Social Structure*. Illinois: The Free Press of Glencoe, 1963. Print.

[ii] It is Letter XVIII in Seneca's work titled: Seneca. *Letters from a Stoic*. New York: Penguin Group, 2004. Print.

> interested in other people's reactions to our practice of poverty. Practicing poverty should help us find something crucial out about what social stratification is. We put on disheveled clothes and spend a few hours sitting around observing what happens.
>
> ➤ "View from above" is an exercise that Pierre Hadot helped to inspire.[iii] Find a quiet spot that is free of distracting noises. Keep your eyes gently closed or you can keep them open. If you keep them open just simply rest them on some object that is not too distracting. Imagine floating above yourself so that you take an aerial view. Now imagine visiting the places that surround the area you live at. Notice what is happening at each of these places.

Stratification is located at the heart of sociology. When we start to look deeply at the society in which we live in, then we can begin to understand that it is indeed greatly stratified. Each society we look at can be stratified in different ways and can have various forms of stratification. Beginning to see that this is so might take some initial effort on our parts (and a little bit of training would not hurt either).

You might turn on the TV and see a commercial that seems to depict a barrage of images of all races, ethnicities, and genders enjoying a brand of clothing or some kind of restaurant food together in happiness and peace. It might give off the impression that things are more "equal" than they have ever been, right? And we could call it a day if we did indeed trust such mass advertising, but we know deep down inside that things are still unequal. So my question is: what is really the problem with this media depiction?

We may live in one region for the remainder of our lives or move to different places with similar circumstances. If this is the case for us, then we may not see how considerably stratified society really is. Sure, we may understand that different people live in different circumstances, but if we keep to our own flock, then it becomes very difficult to really understand and care about what stratification means.

In the beginning of the book, I expressed the benefits of trying to take a social "view from above" (by the way, I really hope you are continuing to practice this exercise every day). We need to begin to think about what is happening in our regions and other regions outside of our own. This is the beginning of cultivating *social compassion*. We try to understand that our society is not at all like a commercial of happy unity. Do we then take a pessimistic view about society as a whole?

As sociologists, we certainly try not to do that. If we did, we might not get too far with our research. There is really too much work that remains to be done! And so, we try to keep our spirits up as best as we can. And we can do this in many different ways. The first, I think, is to recognize that society is greatly stratified. We can do this by attempting to use our sociological imagination to visit places we rarely see and try to witness what is happening there. If suffering is happening there, then we

---

[iii] Hadot, Pierre. *Philosophy as a Way of Life*. Massachusetts: Blackwell Publishing, 1995. Print.

simply look at it and try not to cover it up with silly hegemonic slogans like "well, too bad for them—they did it to themselves!" This way of thinking goes against all that sociology stands for. We attempt to shed light on suffering by noticing it is there and that it is real and that it is larger than just one individual's choices. And we also no longer need to just point the figure at particular groups of people and start a revolution as Karl Marx once thought.

Sociological Thinker

Karl Marx (1818–1883)

Major works: *Communist Manifesto* and *Capital Volume I & II*

Marx was a philosopher and historian who was perhaps the most famous European founder of sociology. His theories have continually influenced sociologists even long after his death. Marx theorized that society was historically driven by class conflict. Each class had its own interests and herein lied the conflict. He noted that capitalism as a system was heading for destruction, and that a revolution would eventually occur, which would finally end all social division. Without social division of class, he argued, we would live in a society that allows people to do what they love.[iv]

What needs to be done is to not only point out these inequalities, which dwell within our society, but rather to begin to develop care and concern about them. What do I mean by this? I am aware that currently some politicians are working for the betterment of people in our society. That seems very legitimate to me to some extent. But what I am talking about here is trying to develop this sociological imagination within our own everyday lives. If you would like to think of America as stratified by class, then please start taking a social "view from above" and go to the upper, middle, working, and lower class areas and see how people are managing there. Use your sociological imagination to spend time in these areas that you would not otherwise visit. It is important for all of us to try and make a real effort to do this in our own lives.

Whatever we do and whatever we happen to think about, that is where we will find our care and concern. If you care about your community, someone might find you organizing and running events in your local neighborhood. If your concern is in shopping, someone might find you enjoying online shopping or traveling to a store near or far from your neighborhood. We can care about these interests of ours and not feel superficial or guilty about them. And why? Because when we begin to develop the sociological imagination, we take moments throughout the day to see how interconnected each aspect of our daily lives are to society. Whether we know it or not, we all help maintain the stratified society in which we live in. In each action, there is a social meaning which is unthought of by us. Can we try and make the unthought-of something worthy of thinking about?

[iv] For more information, please see: Marx, Karl. *The Communist Manifesto*. New York: W. W. Norton & Company, 2013. Print.

One time, when we were studying deviance in class, I was covering Robert Merton's *strain theory*. I was explaining that Merton thinks deviance happens because society tells us the goal we ought to achieve and does not give us equal means to go about achieving it. Merton says that there are five kinds of people we can become in society (and there are really probably more than this). The five kinds of people are the conformist, retreatist, ritualist, innovator, and the rebel.[v] After I finished explaining this to the class, there was a long silence. A young lady then proceeded to raise her hand and I called upon her. She said quite bluntly to the class, "I do not about everyone else, but I do not like my options!" I wholeheartedly concur!

When I tell you that society is stratified and that you maintain this stratification by merely going about your everyday activities, I always receive two types of responses from people. The first is a defeatist attitude that roughly says "this is how it always will be. Nothing we can do will change it." The second response is a some-what self-righteous one and these people usually say to me, "We need to change this situation immediately! What is wrong with you people? Why are you all shopping and consuming mindlessly?" Maybe there is a way we can do our shopping and be conscious about it? And do we need to be consistent with our activism and passivism? These are questions I think are worth asking. Heaven forbid, a student walks away from my sociology class feeling like they have only these two options: give up or join the movement!

Social stratification is a large topic. What it essentially tries to say is that society is divided up into statuses that are normatively ranked from desirable to least desirable. For instance, being poor might be seen by us as an undesirable status. In fact, it is! I ask my students in my classes to tell me what they think the most desirable positions in society are. Most of them tell me the president, CEO's, politicians', a doctor, or other kinds of professions along these lines. Can you write down a list of five positions in society that you find desirable? Does your list look similar to what was mentioned above? If so, what do you think that says about the list itself?

I usually ask my students in rebuttal, "does anyone desire to be poor?" You can probably guess the answer to that question by answering it yourself. Many people might not see being poor as a desirable path in life. And why should they, right? Normatively speaking, it is exactly like my students say, it is completely undesirable. But as we come to find out in sociology, what is undesirable can eventually lead to *stigmatization*.[vi]

When sociologists look at a particular society, they look for these types of things. What is the most prestigious status in society? What is the most powerful status? Are these statuses of prestige and power found within organizations, businesses, corporations, or governmental positions? What is the lowest status in society? How about the intermediate ones? There are many ways to talk about social stratification in sociology, one way, in particular, is to use *surveys*. Surveys are a series of questions intended to be filled out by groups of people. The aim is to collect a surfeit of information in order to be able to say something about those groups of people.

---

[v] Merton, Robert K. *Social Theory and Social Structure*. Illinois: The Free Press of Glencoe, 1963. Print.

[vi] For the reason why this might be so, please see Chapter 6 on labeling theory.

MY STORY OF "PRACTING POVERTY"

When I was over in England, I took to reading a particular philosopher's letters. The philosopher's name was Lucius Annaeus Seneca. Seneca was a Stoic philosopher and he performed many different philosophical exercises within his own life. The letters that he wrote are pieces of philosophical advice that he himself recommends to a friend. One of the philosophical exercises he recommends to his friend is to take a few days each month to live in poverty. At first, this might not sound like the right advice to give to a friend. It might actually seem rather absurd to hear a friend of yours recommending that you practice voluntary poverty monthly. I know I was shocked when I read it.

When I got into the discipline of sociology, I knew that there was a sociological exercise trapped somewhere in Seneca's advice. I also knew by personal experience how demanding the exercise really was! Yes, I actually took up Seneca's advice and slightly amended it, I spent a few hours outside in the cold myself. The question that now faced me was: could I really ask other people to do this exercise without feeling like it was too much in an academic setting? I finally was able to put aside my own self-doubts to amend and tailor this exercise for a sociological fitting. And it now looks good! I hope you will try it on for yourself.

When I first encountered this exercise personally, it seemed somewhat crazy to me as well. After I read the purpose of it, that is, to face our fears and develop foresight so we can prepare ourselves for whatever purported ills may come our way—I thought I might give it a try for myself. I decided not to do this exercise as Seneca recommended it (which means living on the streets for two or three days). Instead, I spent a couple of hours outside in disheveled clothes walking around the city center. I would silently ask myself the question that Seneca recommended keeping in mind, "is this the worst thing that I feared?" The bulk of people would cast their glance away from me and I wondered if this was a norm in Britain to avoid eye-contact in the streets or if it had something to do with my self-imposed status.

By the way, if we are going to talk about statuses once again, then I would like to point your attention to something very peculiar about them. Some statuses develop and enforce what Merton calls a *master status*. Remember how statuses vary according to social context and interaction? Sometimes you are in "brother role," and other times in "relationship role," and even more so, at times you might find yourself in "poet" role. The idea is that some of these statuses and the roles are flexible, and just because you partake in one of them now does not mean you are exclusively known by them when you encounter the first random person you meet. The same cannot be said when you find yourself in a master status. Anyone who encounters you is likely to "know" you exclusively by that status. A master status can be very stigmatizing, especially if the labels that are attached to them are viewed as being deviant and undesirable.

When I performed this particular exercise, I was finding myself inching into a master status. Now since it was a brief experiment, I did not find myself internalizing this master status and the particular roles that come along with it. If I did, then that would be an example of labeling theory and stigmatization.

I would wait outside my favorite little co-op shop in my dirty grey sweatpants that I smeared beforehand with mud. I put a little mud on my face as well and tried to walk differently to get into the role I was attempting to create. Waiting against the wall in this new way was very interesting. I started to notice once again Goffman's civil inattention. People were noticing me without acknowledging me. Some people would catch my eye and then give me space. Sometimes it felt like it was out of respect. Other times, it felt problematic like "oh, great not this type of guy again . . ." After I finished up the exercise, I really understood how developing a master status and being labeled can really affect your life chances and certainly stratify you in undesirable ways.

Assessment/Checklist/Questions

Exercise 1: *Instructions for "practicing poverty"*

- Pick a date and a time where you will have a couple of hours free.
- Choose a spot with a surfeit of people.
- Choose a spot where you can also loiter in peace, that is, a mall or by a train station.
- Find yourself some disheveled clothes to wear. Maybe last week's dirty laundry?
- Leave all your money at home—you will not need it!
- Take some time to sit down, ask people for change, or just walk around.
- Notice what happens.
- You can choose to fast for that day, and only buy food and drink from the money people give you.

Exercise 2: *Instructions for "the view from above"*

- Find a quiet place where noise and distractions are minimal.
- Close your eyes or keep them open.
- Imagine yourself taking an aerial view above yourself.
- While in the aerial view, look around at the area you are currently at.
- When you feel comfortable enough try and "fly" around to other places around the area, that is, go to upper, middle, and lower class areas.
- What are the people doing in each of the areas? What are they saying? How are they interacting? You can "zoom in" and listen to what is happening there.
- If you are having trouble visualizing, you can draw the aerial view on paper and imagine that way.

Focus Questions

- Please write a list of positions you find undesirable in society? Try and list five or so positions. Limit your choices to occupations.

  - Do you think a majority of people would agree with your list? How about your classmates? Go ahead and compare lists.

  - What do you think about the people who occupy these positions? Do they hold power in society? How about any prestige?

  - Do you think undesirable positions are usually always associated with a lower rank? Or can you think of some examples that might dispel that? If so, why do you think some undesirable positions fare better than others?

- Please write a list of positions that you find desirable in society? Try and list five or so positions. Again, focus on occupations.

  - Do you think a majority of people would agree with your list? Do you think they would disagree with you? Why? Why not? Go ahead and compare lists.

  - Do you find that the people who occupy these positions hold some prestige? How about power?

  - What do you think it takes to reach one of those desirable positions? Does it just take years of hard and dedicated work to achieve it? Do some people achieve it without working hard? If so, why do you think that is?

- Exercise 1: "Practice poverty."

  - Keep on the lookout for how people interact with you.

    - How are you being "looked at" by other people? How might this "look" add to labeling theory and stigmatization?

    - What might this have to do with the concept of master status?

    - When other people saw you dressed the way you were and asking for money—do you think they put you into a "role?" What role do you think that was? Do you think it was a positive or negative role?

    - Were you able to make any friends while doing this experiment? Was anybody friendly to you? If so, who was it?

Everyone's "Doing Gender"

8

SUMMARY OF THE MAIN IDEAS

➤ "Doing gender" is a microinteractionist theory developed by Candace West and Don H. Zimmerman.[i] It rejects that gender is something "natural" and it states that we come to know and identify with our genders by practicing them constantly throughout our daily lives.

➤ Social categories are social groups of people that are identified by a multiplicity of characteristics, that is, age, race, ethnicity, sexuality, gender, etc.

➤ Social construction of reality is the idea that we help to socially create the world around us.

➤ Fag discourse is an ethnographic research project carried out in a middleclass high school by C. J. Pascoe.[ii] Pascoe noticed that the boys were policing the boundaries of masculinity by various practices like name calling and aggression toward other boys and girls outside of those boundaries.

SUMMARY OF THE MAIN EXERCISE

➤ "Sweetie/bro vernacular" is a conscious exercise of inverting the language of gender. You use the opposite language for your own gender and vice versa.

---

[i] West, C.; Zimmerman, D. Doing Gender. *Gender & Society*, 1987, 1(2), 125–151.
[ii] Pascoe, C. J. *Dude, You're a Fag: Masculinity and Sexuality in High School*. Berkeley, University of California Press, 2007. Print.

What is gender? How does it affect the lives that we lead? To begin answering this question, you might consider the last restaurant you visited. Perhaps you excused yourself from the table and strolled onward toward the restroom where you saw two stick figures in front of you—which figure did you wind up choosing?

For the rest of the book, we will be spending our time examining some of these *social categories*. Social categories are groups of people who are grouped together by others and share similar characteristics that they identify strongly with. People both in and out of these social categories help legitimatize their identifications by recognizing each other's categories.

Let us start with recalling a few ideas from the previous chapters. Remember Chapter 4 on socialization and the self? Well, in case you are having trouble, I will briefly recap it. Socialization of the self roughly states that we begin to know something about who we are as a person by virtue of simply interacting with other people. And please tell me that you remember the power of groups found in Chapter 5? Yes, it is true that social groups can give us a powerful sense of who we are. But they can also be harmful! Remember when we particularly noticed some of those harmful features in Chapter 6 on social deviance? If other people perceive us negatively, then it can thereby affect the way we perceive ourselves and our own identity. As we continue to progress onward, please make sure to keep these things in mind so that we can continue to build up our sociological imagination.

Gender is a very large topic in the discipline of sociology and a lot has been said about it. In this chapter, we are going to limit ourselves and focus our vision on just getting a small glimpse into the world of gender. We will turn all our attention toward two sociologists in particular, and their names are Candace West and Don Zimmerman. In 1987, they published a famous article together titled "Doing Gender." Their article is a very thought-provoking one, and this is especially so for us, as we try and continue to cultivate our sociological imaginations.

If you are new to sociology, then you may be somewhat unfamiliar with some of its challenges on traditional ideas. These traditional ideas that sociology challenges might seem so utterly "natural" to you. Usually, we might feel that gender is exclusively linked to biology. Sociology, on the other hand, has other insights to offer us that I think are definitely worth being heard and kept in mind.

When I teach on the topic of gender, many of my students seem to think that gender stops at the biological apparatus. It seems as if it is a given and obvious fact. The thought process is: if you have the "man parts," then the masculinity automatically comes along with it, and likewise for the "lady parts." And even then, some people just stop with the male and female genders, and they happen to believe that these are the only two genders that exist! But if you and I reading this were to just stop here and call it quits, then we would not be doing good sociology. We have to try and investigate what these social things mean in our everyday lives.

As you may already know, sociologists tend to examine the everyday things that seem so obvious to everyone. In fact, when we begin to look into gender as a sociologist, we can begin to see what West and Zimmerman were talking about when they wrote that article on "doing gender." And what were they talking about anyways? Well, to some extent we all "do" gender in one way or another. If we can recall our talks in Chapter 3 on culture, then we can begin to further see what this "doing" might mean sociologically. We must practice our culture everyday by choosing to perform it, even if we are not really consciously aware that this is what we are in fact doing. We simply return to ourselves and our ways of doing life and keep them going by practicing them.

In my classes, I often stop and look around the room. I notice that some students are taking notes, some are on the computer typing, others are texting with their phone beneath their desks, and still others are just trying to catch a nap. I like to remind all of them that they are partaking in something I like to call "class culture." And we all partake in this process by doing what we are doing at that moment in time. I mean imagine for just a moment that everybody stopped practicing society. What do you think would happen? What do you think that would look like?

Please allow me to take you back to the beginning scene of this chapter (and I apologize for leaving you standing there all alone at the bathroom door). By the way, time's up: which restroom did you wind up choosing? West and Zimmerman might say your choice is part of an ongoing practice of performing your gender. Sounds a little like Goffman's *dramaturgical theory*, right? It definitely has similarities to it. The idea that we practice our gender and other people help us do so might sound somewhat liberating to you and West and Zimmerman think it should. There is no fixed script that each of us must follow if we have a certain "body part." We are free to choose our gender through our practice of it. This means that gender is fluid and not a fixed thing. Can you see how that might challenge the traditional notion of gender being exclusively fixed and biological?

Now although there is some liberation in this notion, there are also some constraints, and believe me, other people will let you know what those are! That is why understanding deviance becomes so central to the whole of the sociological project. You should always keep that in mind as you do these social exercises of ours.

West and Zimmerman help us understand that each of us continues to work out our gender roles and scripts, and that they are entirely open-ended. Now imagine if all of a sudden you chose to go into the opposite bathroom. And you did this because you felt like the other gender and you just happened to read that gender is a fluid thing that you practice. Would you be practicing the other gender? How do you think people from the other gender would receive you if they saw you? Would they throw a party and welcome you to their big gender family? Would you get a special pin to induct you into their gender family circle? Or would the scene look a little bit uglier than all of that?

Social life is something like a total experience. If we can begin to see this, then we have the second puzzle piece to understanding "doing gender." This key insight is something Peter Berger helped to point out. Berger happened to notice that everything we do in social life is a *social construction of reality*.[iii] What he means by this is that our world is created through the various practices and identifications of social beings interacting with each other. It turns out that we have come to create this whole thing called society! Impressive, right?

Please take a moment to write down a list of ways in which you think you might practice doing your gender? Is it by choosing to dress in the way you do? Is it because

---

[iii] Berger, P.; Luckmann, T. *The Social Construction of Reality: A Treatise in the Sociology of Knowledge*, Garden City, NY: Anchor Books, 1966. Print.

you listen to particular kinds of music? Watch certain TV shows? How about the way you kiss another person? Please try and write down five or so practices of doing gender in your daily routine.

I have a special exercise for you to perform when you can find the time to do it adequately. I call it "the sweetie/bro vernacular." It is really easy to do it and everyone is welcome to try it out for themselves to see the results. We are going to try to narrow our scope down to the way we create gender through language. Besides expressing ourselves through fashion, actions, and a whole array of different things, we can manage to raise a few eyebrows with just the slightest deviation in our own language.

We will try and "do gender" by practicing the opposite expressions of our gender. So say you view yourself as a man and you continue to practice "doing man" by the various ways you interact with other people. I suggest you start to call members of your gender "sweetie," "darling," or "girlfriend" and see what happens when you do so. It is always best to do this exercise out in a public setting, that is, a café of some kind. When the cashier rings you up (and should he be a man), go on and thank him by saying "thanks sweetie."

Whatever gender you happen to identify as, be sure to practice the opposite language. It might sound a little stupid at first, but try and pretend you are the other gender when you associate with the cashiers. I have found that it helps to use body language to get into character. If we are all actors and actresses playing roles in society, then it might not be that difficult for you to figure out how to practice playing the opposite gender. Try it out for yourself!

When you do this exercise, you can practice using this language on five or so people to begin with, and it is best if they are strangers working behind a cash register. And I will tell you why I have found this strategy to be best in just a moment.

This exercise is essentially not about identifying with the gender you are using the language for (but if you do, then by all means please do!). I do not expect people to become the opposite sex when they construe these utterances. Come on, I am just a sociology teacher, not a sorceress or sorcerer. That would be asking for a bit too much on my part! What I would like you to see is that this language is gender specified because of its continual usage and practice in our own everyday lives.

When other people look at you strange and give you a double take, then you know that on the canvas of society you have splattered some kind of neon colored paint all over the societal portrait. And we all know something is quite off when language does not function as it usually does. This impediment is the perfect chance for you to examine what it means to practice gender in a linguistic and idiosyncratic kind of way.

I also would like you to be careful when you attempt this exercise. Language both verbal and bodily, when used in ways people deem inappropriate, can be very dangerous. I have been threatened before by men when I called them "sweetie." If something like this happens to you, then please know when to quit. You might want to apologize to the person or tell them it was just a social experiment. If both of these do not appeal to them, then you might wish to do as a British cop once told me and "just walk away."

What you should not do is play devil's advocate to someone who is frustrated. In the case of the man who threatened me, sociologist C.J. Pascoe's *fag discourse* was all too clear to me. Pascoe mentions that men may police the borders of masculinity and protect it through the use of social cues (bodily and verbal language). This can sometimes take the form of harassing other people who happen to fall right on the borderline or outside the border of masculinity. This is where that man was indeed locating me when he threatened me.

MY STORY OF USING THE "SWEETIE/BRO VERNACULAR"

I first started assigning this exercise about a year ago. First, as always, I had to try and do it for myself and see if I had any success with it.

I would occasionally slip a "sugar" or "hun" to close friends of mine. My friends just laughed at me and did not take it serious at all. So I asked myself: would random strangers have the same reaction that my friends had on me? I decided to try this vernacular on strangers of the same gender who I happened to have some kind of social encounter with. As I mentioned before, my friends would just laugh it off nonchalantly. Strangers, however, would often give me a double take, smirk, or say something back to me to let me know that I was doing something "wrong."

I should mention that I was in a small rural area when I did this exercise. The area itself was also rather conservative. I am bound to at least see about five confederate flags as I drive to this rural town. So I think it is probably a good idea to really consider where you are before performing this exercise. Also, it might be worthwhile to consider the "general mood" of the place before undertaking any further action. If it looks like it is filled with a bunch of Client Eastwood types, then you are better off trying a different place.

Anyways, as I was walking around this small quaint town, a gentleman had a question for me and approached me in my general direction. I figured that this might be a good enough time to practice this exercise and act out a subtle femininity in both my language and body. You are probably thinking that I changed the tone of my voice and so forth. Nope, not so! Recall that I said *subtle*, and that is the way I kept it. And I suggest you keep your differences as subtle as possible. Please do not exaggerate this exercise. There is no need to go over the top with your acting like Jim Carey.

The conversation seemed cordial enough (even with my subtle mannerisms) until I said "thanks sweetie." A glitch in the matrix occurred for a moment and then he immediately took up arms by saying "what did you call me!?" And he began to come closer to me in haste. I told him I was a sociology professor doing a social experiment and backed away from him. I sort of hopped back. He never asked me "what is the experiment for?" The tense moment soon dissolved between us as I walked away and it was like the whole thing never happened. I turned back in his general direction and it turned out he was not following me; he was speedily walking in the other direction.

As I sat in my car, I began recording the event in my journal. I noticed the problems that come with practicing gender. These problems run up against a strong history of what we (me and others included) think gender should be like. And this is especially strange for me since "we all create and practice this social thing together!"

Assessment/Checklist/Questions

Exercise 1: *Instructions for the "sweet/bro vernacular"*

- Go to a public place.
- Be conscious of your surroundings.
- Survey the general mood of the place.
- Do not force the interaction (I suggest enacting this approach with a cashier).
- Act as the opposite gender in both body and verbal language (do this subtly).
- Be on the lookout for responses from other people.
- If you are in danger, then walk away!

Focus Questions

- In your journal, please put up a division between "the social" and "the biological" and list a couple of things that you think fall under one or the other.
  - Are there some things on your list that you think fall under both categories? If so, what are they?
  - Please consider what it means to say that everything we "do" is a social construction?
    - What do you think it would mean for us if we adopted this idea when we thought about our own gender and sexuality?
    - What if we all stopped "practicing" our genders?
- Please take a moment to think about what Candace West and Don H. Zimmerman said. What are some of the ways that you "do gender" in your daily life?
  - You can go through your daily routine and write a couple of things down. Maybe start with five things or so.
  - Look over the list and figure out how practicing your gender might affect what you do and how you do it.
  - What are some choices you continually make in order to preserve your own gender? Please provide some examples.
- Exercise 1: "Sweetie/bro vernacular."
  - What happened when you acted and spoke like the opposite gender? How did you act? What did you say? Do you really think that the opposite gender really acts that way?
  - Did people feel awkward?
  - How did you feel while doing this exercise?
  - Do you feel that the person expected you to be more like a certain gender? If so, what does that say about gender and the "looking glass self?"

Learning Privileges in the Race

9

SUMMARY OF THE MAIN IDEAS

➤ Race is an arbitrary characteristic that sets a social group of people apart. It is a social construction and it varies in characteristic across both cultural space and time.

➤ White privilege is something that Peggy McIntosh's article "White Privilege: Unpacking the Invisible Knapsack" helped bring into focus.[i] White privilege is unearned advantages that pertain to a particular race in social, cultural, political, and economic spheres.

➤ "Double consciousness" is a concept that W. E. B. Dubois helped bring into focus.[ii] It involves having to read and act from two different scripts in a variety of different social contexts. One script is the act of performing the appropriate norm in that particular context and the other script is the awareness that you may be targeted by other social actors with a prejudicial bias.

SUMMARY OF THE MAIN EXERCISES

➤ "List your privileges" is a writing exercise. Just mull over some possible privileges you have over other people. You can start with whether you can see or not, whether you can walk or not, and so forth. I would ultimately like you to try and think of your race, ethnicity, gender, or sexuality privileges.

---

[i] McIntosh, P. *White Privilege and Male Privilege: A Personal Account of Coming to See Correspondences through Work in Women's Studies*. Wellesley, MA: Wellesley College Center for Research on Women, 1988.
[ii] Dubois, W. E. B. *The Souls of Black Folk*. Paris: A. C. McClurg & Co, 1903.

➤ "Reflection on intersection" is a weeklong exercise that consists in waking up and examining the intersection of your race, class, and gender on society. I am indebted to Naomi Miller for advising me of this particular exercise.

What is it like to practice seeing our racial and ethnic privileges? What constitutes a privilege? And what part do privileges play in understanding our historical social categories? In this chapter, we will explore some of these questions and more.

Let's try and begin with defining what we mean when we talk about race. Many people might define race as being a physical characteristic that is exclusively linked to our biology. This way of thinking about race is often called *essentialism*. This viewpoint stresses that because a phenomenon exists as it does now (in our case whatever race we are discussing), it has always existed as such. In other words, there is some kind of *essence* to this phenomenon that is unchanging.

We can easily see how this kind of thinking can be somewhat dangerous to adopt in the world we live in today. I think this is partly because essentialism tends to confuse social phenomena with biological ones. Race as a social phenomenon is a historically changing process that varies across time and place. This is an important thing to remember. Please try and keep it in mind as best you can as we continue on. As sociologists, we study history, culture, and society. And this helps us uncover the reality that race is really an historical social construction that is maintained by institutions, social categories and groups. These social groups often set people apart based on (and not always) physical differences.

To sum it up: we have seen two differing ideological views. The first being that of race viewed through the notion of essentialism. This idea refuses to acknowledge the created past of our social history and how it affects how we currently think today. The second kind of thinking is sociological. When we do this kind of thinking, we begin to understand that the forces of our social history continue to affect us even today. So what now? If we continue to merely talk about the ideological differences between these concepts, then we might miss the real-life consequences of these thought processes.

Let us now spend a little time thinking about some real-life consequences of the social category of race in action. In 2014, a young man named Rashad Polo[iii] happened to post a controversial video on Vine. In the video, Polo documents a real-life occurrence of what it means to "shop while black." He records an actual occurrence of racism as he walks around the convenience store while being closely followed by a white woman. This mode of awareness was given the name *double consciousness* and it was a concept developed in 1903 by W. E. B. Dubois in his book *The Souls of Black Folk*. Basically, it means that nonwhites and minority groups will have to follow at least two different kinds of scripts while in various societal contexts. The first script is

---

[iii] Follow this link to see the video which features Polo's Vine post. https://www.youtube.com/watch?v=q32NhDy4ZQg

the one that we all would follow and it can simply be called the normative script. The second script, however, is paying close attention to the fact that you might be under prejudicial scrutiny by several fellow bystanders. This insight leads us into privilege.

As a white man, I walk around the grocery store and sometimes eat my food as I shop. I get hungry while I shop, don't you? I open up granola bar boxes and throw them in my cart. As I do it, and Phil Collins plays in the background for the hundredth time, I seemingly have no cares at all in the world. I have never actually experienced a fellow scrutinizing bystander. I have even walked by security guards and done this! In fact, I do not even have to think at all about how my whiteness will conjure up negative images in other people's heads. I do not really have to think about race at all in this situation. Isn't that somewhat unbelievable? For me, this is an example of an unearned privilege that I experience in my own daily life.[iv] What do you think are some other privileges that I might experience because I am white? Please take a moment or two to jot a few down.

In her now famous article, Peggy McIntosh writes on the subject of privilege, and more specifically, on how white privilege affects our everyday interactions. She attempts to observe some of her own privileges that she meets with throughout her day. McIntosh is entirely aware that within her own life she often forgets these privileges. If someone who studies these things as a scholar can forget them, then so can we! So once you begin to practice identifying some of your daily privileges, I would advise you to be as gentle with yourself as possible if you find yourself forgetting your privileges. Forgetting is a part of everyday life, and when we find ourselves forgetting, we can take some time to remember. I would say the best way to remember is to make an effort to remember. You really have to set aside some time to practice thinking about your privileges. What are they? I will touch on all this a little bit later on when we come to the exercises, but for right now, it is just enough to mention it here.

I have a friend who was studying to become a grade school teacher. Anyways, this friend was highly upset when she had to learn about white privilege in her classes. She said, "Enough is enough! I get it! Whites are more privileged than non-whites. Can we please move on to the good stuff like child psychology? I really want to learn what kids are thinking about these days." I have met a lot of people who feel a similar way about the subject of privilege. It is often met adversely or seen as such an obvious subject that it really merits no ongoing study.

In fact, I taught a course on Majority–Minority relations and most of the people in class seemed to act like they were some kind of a race scholar majoring in the area of privilege. This makes sense, since race is a concept that we all seem to know in one way or another and it seems obvious enough to us.

In my class, it was repeatedly brought to my attention over and over again that once we defined what privilege was, we could then move on to the better stuff. This is it though! This is what we are trying to work on when we talk about race in this chapter!

What I started to notice in my classes was the concept of "whiting out" issues on race and gender. This is something that fascinated me. As we got deeper into

---

[iv] This example is also used and stated somewhat differently in Dalton Conley's textbook *You May Ask Yourself.*

discussions on how a multiplicity of factors affect all of our lives, students would then bring the discussion back to Marxist class issues. What would begin to emerge among the most opinionated of my students was dominant ideologies of "work ethic" and basic class issues of laziness. I noticed that this "whiting out" attempted to erase real issues of intersectionality among the social categories by simply removing them.

I was frustrated about the whole matter of privilege and so I went to my department chair and asked her for some advice. My question was: why was privilege being seen by students as something easy to understand and yet it seemed that we all were missing the point. She told me it is their privilege not to know what privilege is!

I struggled long and hard with these questions by myself. I was now in a position to teach privilege and how it affects other people's lives, and it is real both culturally and institutionally. And I also had to often deal with white students who felt it was their duty to make themselves seem as non-normative as possible through their lived-experience, either that or they felt that they were constantly under attack in the classroom when we talked about these subjects of privilege. It seemed like they felt "whiteness" was under attack. I frequently thought of the 1980s hardcore group Minor Threat and their song "Guilty of Being White," where the lead singer wants to be viewed as being far removed from earlier racist times. The problem is that we cannot remove ourselves from history. There is so much suffering in the history of race. All this suffering did not happen overnight and it will not cease at the end of the day either. And if we are not careful as people, then we can begin to feel hostile and annexed from it. The suffering can be overwhelming. We do not want to be blamed for something many of us feel we had no part of, but as sociology repeatedly tells us: larger historical forces continually shape our lives even at this very hour. In this chapter, we are going to focus on these forces in the form and shape of race and privilege.

The white students are especially always in danger of taking white privilege in bad faith. If white students feel turned off by all of it, then we can get nowhere in our discussions on how their very race affects the lives of all of us and vice versa! This is not to single out particular races. For a long time, whiteness was invisible as a category and everything else stood out as different and deviant. Now with white studies currently underway, we are finally making this social category visible.

It seems to me that white people need to start caring about racial issues and begin to take them seriously. I see this as one of the major issues in our times. In my classes, I ask my students whether they think racism can end or not. I immediately receive many emphatic "no's!" Many students are highly convinced that what I am asking for is in fact impossible. They told me we have a much better shot at discovering another earth, traveling to it and inhabiting it rather than ending racial conflict in the United States. Do we really think that these issues of race are entirely unsolvable? And do we really think that finding another earth to inhabit seems more probable than solving these issues of race? It felt ridiculous to me to write those last few sentences.

I also asked my students, "Do you often think about how we can end racism or not?" They usually continue the emphatic response with a one-word answer, "no." It turns out that they do not really think about the question at all. I wonder why. Is the question of whether or not racism can end a question that deserves our attention in these times? Really, I would like you to think about whether or not it matters at all.

It seems to me that we need to start cultivating care about race and issues of racism. The question becomes: how do we cultivate this care? And I think dwelling on our privileges and the privileges of others as well as the question on whether or not it is possible for racism to end are a few ways to begin to cultivate this care.

So talking about privilege is a very difficult thing to do, especially in an artificial classroom setting, but that does not mean it is an impossible undertaking. I would just like the reader to understand this point especially, and also see that we are not working toward a definition of privilege. Definitions tend to finish things. And whatever is finished is not considered worthy of our thoughts. We have to keep things open and continue the ongoing investigation into our own personal privileges within the intersection of these social categories.

I have a number of sociological exercises on race that have come to my attention from various sources and I would like to share them all with you. Before we come together to discuss the topic of race, please try and give yourself at least one week to practice one of these exercises daily. I am always partial to doing them in sequential order, but please feel free to explore each of them in whatever order that happens to suit you best. Try and enjoy the benefits of developing a consciousness that meditates on race actively. Many of us may have the privilege to forget about it. But let us be gentle enough to ourselves as we begin our study on our privileges.

Whenever you get a couple of minutes to yourself out of your busy schedule, and the time is ample enough for you to collect and compose yourself in a suitable manner, then please allow yourself to settle in and grab your notebook. If it happens to be a beautiful day outside, then perhaps you would like to find a comfortable space to sit down and write. I personally enjoy writing on the train station steps. I especially like this spot when it is seemingly abandoned, and not a single person can be found. I enjoy setting my sights on the distant railroad tracks and writing. A beautiful place like this can help us think and write. I would suggest finding yourself a similar place that might inspire you to write. Try and treat the place as if it were a conversing friend.

The first practice I will explicate is a simple and powerful writing exercise. As I mentioned before, I find this to be the best place to begin on the subject. The exercise derives itself from the wisdom contained in Peggy McIntosh's essay on privilege. We are to take a few moments every day and write down a list of our privileges as we experience them throughout the day and how they might affect other people. We can start by asking ourselves if it is it an earned or unearned privilege. You might want to start with trying to write at least five. I would like them to be about your race, but if you are stumped by this, then please feel free to start as general as possible. Here is what I mean: if you can walk, then you might experience what is called "walking privilege" in a building that has no elevator or walkway.

I would just like you to become familiar with what a privilege is, what it means to experience it as such, and how it may affect other people around you. When you start writing up your list, you might begin to see part of your experience that was always there, but remained unthought-of by you. Being handicapped is still part of the non-normative experience and many of the buildings and places that we visit were designed for use by "normative persons."

Once you have your list written down and you have spent ample time returning to it daily (approximately a week, but please feel free to continue indefinitely!), then you can begin to move on to the second exercise. In this practice, which was explained to me most kindly by a friend and colleague of mine (Naomi Miller) and was done so at the request of having a practice for the students to do that would help us all see intersectionality much clearer.

Please allow me to briefly pause in order to explain the term intersectionality. It was in existence as early as the 19th century, but it was finally given a name in the 1980s by Kimberlé Williams Crenshaw. Intersectionality aims to view how our social categories link themselves to power and oppression in culture, historical social structures, and stratums of society.

Naomi Miller suggested a practice that she frequently performs on a daily basis. We might just give it the name "reflection on intersection" to save ourselves the embarrassment of just calling it "Exercise 2." So when doing "reflection on intersection," we wake up in the morning and as we approach the mirror we thoughtfully try and see how our race, class, gender, ethnicity, age, and other social categories intersect with each other and how they, in turn, effect society.

The third and final exercise that I will mention was also inspired by a fellow colleague of mine. Stacie Golin sent me a link to a standup comedian's routine; the comedian's name is Aamer Rahman.[v] I will provide the link in the next section for those who are interested in watching this talented comedian's exposition of the exercise. Meanwhile, I will just summarize what the exercise entails. Many people I know wonder why white people cannot say the "n-word" in even a jesting manner. Think for a moment about the controversy surrounding Michael Richards when he used the "n-word" during a standup comedy performance.

To help us understand why white people may not say potentially offensive things like this, but nonwhites may be able to get away with it—a notion which has been dubbed "reverse racism"—Rahman explains the disparity, I think, rather clearly. He says: imagine if instead of Europeans experiencing the industrial boom, going out and colonizing the world, taking over their resources, exploiting them, and subjecting the world to their standards and ideals, it went the other way instead. What if Africa and Asia grouped together to take over Europe? What if they sold Europeans into slavery and exploited their resources and land? What if, after years of oppression toward whites, an African man went on a comedy stage and said "what is it with white people anyways—why can't they dance?" According to Rahman, that would be an example of real reverse racism!

Assessment/Checklist/Questions

Exercise 1: *Instructions for "listing your privileges"*

- Please think about some of your unearned privileges.
- If you are having trouble thinking about some of your own unearned privileges, turn to Peggy McIntosh's article "White Privilege: Unpacking the Invisible Knapsack" online (https://www.isr.umich.edu/home/diversity/resources/white-privilege.pdf) or Jewel Woods article "Black Male Privileges Checklist" online

---

[v] Follow this link to view the video: https://www.youtube.com/watch?v=dw_mRaIHb-M

(http://www.deanza.edu/faculty/lewisjulie/The%20Black%20Male%20 Privilege%20Checklist.pdf); either way, you might be able to get some ideas on your own privileges by referring to these lists.

- Write down at least five of your own privileges that your experience daily.

Exercise 2: *Instructions for "reflection on intersection"*

- Every morning for one week: as you wake up, be sure to look in the mirror or take a moment to envision yourself.
- You can "envision yourself" by closing your eyes and visualizing each of your social categories. You can start with your race and then move onto how it intersects with your gender and continue onward until you understand how they all relate to each other.
- Once you have really visualized or thought about your social categories and how they relate. I advise you to meditate further by answering some of the following questions:
- What is my race, class, gender, and sexuality?
- How do they all intersect with each other to make up who I am? How much identity do I invest in each of these social categories? For example, am I more invested in how I sexually identity than in how I racially identify?
- How does my identity help create other peoples' identities? Can my "whiteness" exist alone without other races?
- How do these social categories affect my life chances?
- How do they affect other peoples?
- How are other people valuing these social categories? What is the default category? How do I matchup with that ideal?
- Please down your reflections in your journal.
- At night, replay the course of your day and think about how your identification to the social categories has affected it.

Exercise 3: *Instructions on "reversing history"*

- Watch Aamer Rahman's comedy sketch on "reverse racism" here: https://www. youtube.com/watch?v=dw_mRaIHb-M
- Imagine if history was altered and Europeans did not colonize a good portion of the world, but instead it went the other way and non-Europeans took over the majority of the world's resources.
- Imagine further that non-Europeans subjected Europeans to a slave trade.
- Committed further acts like oppression, exploitation, and subjected their own ethnocentric standards and values on the Europeans.
- Then imagine a non-European making fun of a European. Can you begin to see "reverse racism" in this sense?

Focus Questions

- What is the difference between thinking of race through an essentialist point of view versus a social constructivist?
  - Please draw a Venn diagram to help you see differences and similarities.
  - Define the key elements of each pattern of thought.
  - Create an example for each of them.
  - What is the overlap? What are the differences?
  - More importantly, which style of thinking are you more "at home" in performing? Why? And how do you think this effects the way we think about race?
- Watch Rashad Polo's video on "shopping while black" (https://www.youtube .com/watch?v=q32NhDy4ZQg).
  - What do you think about the video? Race definitely matters, why is this instance potentially stigmatizing?
  - Please explain why this is a real-life example of double consciousness?
  - Have you ever gone to a place where you needed to exercise double consciousness? If so, where was it? And what context was it in?
- Exercise 1: List your privileges.
  - How do these privileges affect your daily life?
  - Do all people receive these privileges you wrote down? Which ones are exclusive to you?
  - How might your privilege affect other people in everyday life?
- Exercise 2: Reflection on intersection.
  - Reflect as you are reflecting by asking some of these questions:
    - What is my race, class, and gender?
    - How do they all intersect with each other to make up who I am?
    - How does my identity help create other peoples'?
    - How do these social categories affect my life chances?
    - How do they affect other peoples?
  - Please write down your reflections in your journal.
  - At night, replay the course of your day.
    - How has your race, class, and gender affected you throughout the day?
    - What are some of the ways they intersected? For example, do you think you just see someone as "a man" and not "a white man?" Do you think you see someone as just "ugly" and not as "an upper class man?"

Concluding Remarks: FAQ in the Back

10

This has been a concise work of mine dealing with how to practice sociology within your own life. I hope you have thoroughly enjoyed your practice of sociology. As you practice more and more, your awareness of the social world should expand, and I believe social compassion will result as a consequence of this awareness.

I hope that this book was able to provide a nice starting point for your practice, and I do hope that you will continue doing these experiments on your own in the same sociological spirit that brought you to this subject in the first place.

I wanted to mention that just because you have done the exercises once or twice, that does not excuse you from the work itself. We have to keep doing these exercises, over and over again, in order to keep the sociological imagination fresh and active.

Sociology is pretty much like any other art that you practice, the emphasis, of course, being on *practice*! We have to really try and put in the time and effort to get the most out of our practice. We are essentially attempting to understand something that is so ordinary and common to us in our own social experiences. When we take a look at these social theories and their obviousness, we might feel like we totally understand them and are in no need of further instruction. I think this is where the danger lies. I have many students who feel like one sociology class is all you need in order to understand the subject. This brash attitude can really stop us from making progress in seeing the theories in the social exercises. Please be weary of this!

I do hope you not only take up these exercises weekly, but perhaps become creative enough to develop some of your own as you continue your interest in the discipline. There are plenty more ways that we can practice doing sociology in our lives. It is always advisable to spend some time reading and hanging out with the classic theorists. From there, you can choose to work your way into the more modern ones. I think this is always a good point of departure for anyone interested in the material because most of what has been said builds off these foundational thinkers. It would be like trying to start with G.W.F. Hegel without first reading Immanuel Kant, or even Aristotle and Plato!

A lot of the thinkers you encounter along the way owe a great deal to the ones that came before them. Of course that does not mean that the dialog starts and ends with these foundational thinkers; it means, rather, that the dialog is always open-ended and ongoing. We would be wise, however, to first pay heed to what has already been said, that way we can build off of what previous thinkers said and address the current issues that we face within our own lives.

Speaking of authority figures, I hope you realize that this book has not attempted in any way to be an authority on the subject of sociology itself. My hopes were invested in the notion that the book might act as a good basis for practicing what it might be like to live a sociological life. It is actually to this end that I have directed all my efforts with producing this book and the manner in which I hope it is received. Thank you all for your patience in listening to what has been said and your attempts at practicing it!

FAQ IN THE BACK

At the close of this book, I would like to take a few minutes to answer any potential questions that readers might have. To this end, I have asked myself a series of questions that I have often encountered while implementing this approach to students. I think it is a good reference guide for students and readers to peruse at their own leisure. It is an especially good source for me personally, as I will now have a text written that I can refer students to and therefore save some precious class time.

Here Are a List of Questions

1. Who are you? What qualifies you to say these things?
2. Isn't this like that one TV show?
3. What kind of success have you had with these sociological exercises?
4. How do you know the students actually do the exercises?
5. Why do you do the exercises yourself?
6. Why is this a good method and approach to adopt while teaching sociology?
7. I have anxiety—do I still have to do the exercises?
8. What if for some reason I cannot do one of the exercises? Will I then not be sociological enough?
9. Why do I have to do these exercises?

1. Who are you? What qualifies you to say these things?

I am glad you asked. There is not enough space to really get into "who I am," but I am guessing what really matters most in the question is the sociological-ness of my credentials. I have taught *Introduction to Sociology* courses at a few colleges and I have immensely enjoyed the experience of doing it. I originally thought I would not enjoy it, as I also have a strong affinity for philosophy, and in some regard, I have been highly influenced by philosophy itself.

In this book's case, I am obviously very influenced by Pierre Hadot's *Philosophy as a Way of Life*. Hadot interprets the ancient philosophical tradition as a "way of life" to be taken up by the practitioner. In this vein, he introduces us to a few of the practices that philosophers took up in order to transform their lives. There were some very compelling philosophical schools with competing views and practices, but ultimately they all agreed that the goal of life was to immerse yourself in the practice itself.

Many of us here at university are somewhat far removed from this sense of practicing. We might not think it is beneficial to practice the thing that we are studying. We tend to look at a course as a place where we will probably listen to a bunch of lectures, read enough just to get by, and memorize what we need to in order to pass the exams. I usually ask my students, "why are you taking my sociology course?" Many students often reply to me in an unenthused tone, "to fill an elective." This answer seems to be monopolizing my sociology courses! Hearing this answer as a professor can be a very sobering experience. I tend to forget that many students sitting in my class are somatically there to fill an elective. It is nothing personal to me or the material, it is just the business of obtaining credentials, and that is something that Randall Collins helped me understand.

There are also places I teach at where the university builds laptop fees into tuition. When I enter into these classrooms and institutions, I have to remember I am now a part of this laptop culture. And it can also be very difficult and downright absurd to ask every student for their undivided attention! To ask students to focus on one subject (that they might not even care about to begin with) for an extended and fixed amount of time—be it an hour or even possibly longer—might truly be asking for something impossible. There is no way I can monopolize their attention on something that might not even captivate their interest in the slightest bit, nor could I rely explicitly on my own articulated discourse, or even the fancy textbook that I use. Plus add the fact that a computer is ready-at-hand before them, all of this—how can I compete with it?

I have to figure out ways to entertain and amuse while in front of students. I find myself dabbling into the comedic arts at times, and I constantly move around, occasionally dancing to stir up the sterility of the dusty room and the serious dispositions that fill it. All of these ways of amusement help draw me closer to whomever it is that is in my presence, and of course, it helps to have these seemingly awkward sociological exercises ready-at-hand. As I mentioned previously, I have been at this teaching thing for about a year and a half. I feel there has been enough time for me to figure out what works and what does not. I am much kinder to myself and others around me, especially with what I ask for.

It is for this reason that I took up journaling with the students. They come to work twice a week or maybe only once, and they should have performed the sociological exercise for that week and written down their experiences. Not only that, but they are expected to finish the notes on that week's readings, which are also written. And they are also asked to take down class notes for the day.

About the readings that I assign to the students, I know there is a certain fixed quota for every college, but I have decided to keep the readings brief. I went to college myself. An unreasonable amount of attention is placed on the privilege of the text. Also, many of these textbooks contain terrible prose writers! Where do all these banal writers come from anyways? Good reading, in my own experience, is never how much you read, but how thoughtful it has made you. That is why even during the assigned portions of the readings, I will ask my students to stop if they feel that a

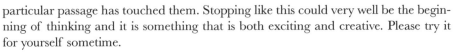

particular passage has touched them. Stopping like this could very well be the beginning of thinking and it is something that is both exciting and creative. Please try it for yourself sometime.

Generally, if you have 40–70 pages to read for all your classes, something like this experience I am talking about will be fleeting. Reading will most likely turn into, "when is this damn section going to end?" or "I give up. Who cares?!" This fleeting feeling is dangerous to me. Over the years, as you read more and more, especially if you are a scholar or academic, it sort of numbs you. It often takes something beautifully textual or nontextual to get you out of that dark void of numbness. I have been there myself. I discourage this ascetic reading lifestyle to the utmost. I would not wish any student to fall down that dark void of numbness over reading. It is definitely good to read (I think we can all agree on that), but a limit is always necessary to observe. Often colleges as institutions, and teachers as archons, use this sort of immoderate tyranny against their attendees and it can be dangerous to the learning experience.

So who am I? Apparently someone who takes a long time to answer a question. I am definitely a protector of creativity, a granter of space, and a forgiving and passionate person who remembers what unnecessary suffering can feel and look like. I hope something of what I've said resonates in your own path of thinking.

2. Isn't this like that one TV show?

Many students ask me this question. I think it is a way to connect the sociological exercises with their own encounters of non-normative behavior. The show I hear most referenced is something called *Impractical Jokers*; this is a show where actors are to engage in silly antics that come across as non-normative behavior. I believe they have a headpiece in their ear and are to follow orders by these seemingly disembodied voices that are comedic and humorous in tone. The show is scripted and contains actors performing roles; it certainly sounds sociological, right?

I am always encouraged by students to watch this show for myself, but I never do. I have to explain fundamental differences for the sake of the reader, who may relate this kind of entertainment to the work we are trying to do here.

Impractical Jokers is first off not practical. The idea is sort of like a prank. These prank shows are gaining popularity, in that they provide humorous relief from the socialness and normalness of everyday life. The aesthetic idea of getting inside of someone's head and telling them to do your humorous biddings amid an audience that loves and supports this kind of entertainment is really a bizarre thing. There is seemingly no direction to the prank and it just runs alongside itself with whatever is presented to it at the moment. The mood of the show itself contains a comicality that continues to present itself artificially, and it plays the prank for a show's length of 30 or so minutes. The joke continual repeats itself and no one seems to be in any "real danger." Many people laugh because the presentation of the program is such that it is something humorous to laugh at.

But enough on *Impractical Jokers*, I assume they were not inspired by the writings of Harold Garfinkel or any other sociologist who uses these types of "breaching experiments" to create space between the normalness of the social and the critical understanding that needs to constantly critique it.

The show works because it has no direction. My sociological exercises, on the other hand, contain direction. This is led by a basic social theory to look for and questions that are tailored to guide us on that looking path. There is of course the additive element that no studio audience will find what you are doing to be comical at all. And as you do each social experiment, you will find this out for yourself. This is not the stage for comedy. Nor will you find humor in being placed in a situation that willfully breaks some informal norms while other people are not expecting it. You might have to announce yourself as a student or a sociological researcher in order to free yourself from potential jeer or danger. Anyways, in your "social life," you must be cognizant of this disparity. It is more "real" and therefore more danger-ous than the stage set on any TV show.

3. What kind of success have you had with these sociological exercises?

This might be a question that a fellow instructor poses to me. I will briefly say that the success has been welcomed due to it being a serious part of the course grade. I take the sociological exercises very seriously. As I mentioned before, I do not privi-lege reading the text over doing the exercises. I like to grant everything a place that is potentially useful for our enterprise.

One of the reasons that students enjoy doing these exercises is the fact that they do not take long to do them. They can be performed very quickly and the questions can be answered just as easily. They are simple enough and accessible to most any-one with an adventurous spirit. It is also the part of the homework that tells you "to go outside and play!"

4. How do you know the students actually do the exercises?

I have students keep a written or typed journal that curtails their experiences while doing the exercises. Generally, there are questions that need answering, but there is also a personal experience that should be recorded as well. I frequently check jour-nals to make sure everyone is on the right track, and I give feedback in instances where I have found weak efforts on the student's part. Usually, I find these "weak efforts" far and few in between. As I mentioned earlier on, many of the students dis-play eagerness to do something outside of the classroom. We try and take sociology to the streets.

5. Why do you do the exercises yourself?

I do the exercises out of consideration and love for the work and for the students. I used to run track in both college and high school. I always appreciated a coach that would run with us, as well as, coach us—it is that age old adage: lead by example. This is what I am attempting to do here in my classroom. I always share my experi-ences of each of the exercises that I perform; I try to give out encouragement for those who are struggling to do them.

In any course that I teach, I feel that we are all trying to work together for the potential to think in an entirely new way. This is very hard work! But I think we all must try our best and do it—that is also why I encourage friendship in my classes.

I would like to tell you personally that I am often scared when I do these exercises by myself. I would like you to realize that I suffer too. On the first day of class, we usually go out together and do a social exercise as a group. In an instance like this, we usually perform the "do nothing" exercise together. I find that when we do this socially awkward thing together as a class, then it really bonds us all together.

6. Why is this a good method and approach to adopt while teaching sociology?

Sociology is a discipline that is eager to have people understand their everyday social lives. Many of these insights go unnoticed by us as we casually continue on with our daily lives. There are some real consequences to some of these sociological insights that can really hurt people. If we continue to just think we have mastered our everyday lives or that they are not really worthy of our attention, then many of these injustices and oppressions will continue to thrive. Sociological awareness, that is, awareness of your own social life, is the crux of enlightenment to help others including yourself. You could potentially be harming someone without even knowing it! That, I think, demands serious reflection on our parts!

This ethnomethodology is really a "method for the people," and it is for our own well-being; I would also like to add that it will help us flourish. We need to see keenly what is happening in our own mundane lives. Once we understand it, we can transform it. Yesterday, a former student and I were outside practicing "doing nothing." We sat down for 20 minutes on the campus green. It was a very beautiful day outside. The sun was tranquilized by the wind, you know, just the right amount of mixture so as not to become too overbearingly hot. After about 20 minutes or so were up, we stood up together and just looked at the campus and the people coming and going. We stood around in this state of presence for nearly four hours! We picked up trash around campus and sent good cheer to those who happened to come along our way. It is so very beautiful to be fully present and know you are living in a social world. The sociological imagination can help us become more present in our own lives, and these exercises are really the key to developing it. We both enjoyed our day together in peace by helping our social environment, and the traces of joy were written all over our actions.

7. I have anxiety—do I still have to do the exercises?

It is okay to be anxious. I am very anxious myself. I remember exactly how class life felt for me. Many teachers would call on me and I would just freeze up. I would become so embarrassed in my diffidence and some of these teachers would sort of make fun of me in their own way for not doing the readings. I did the readings, of course, but when I am called on in the middle of nowhere I get so startled and shake. I never had the courage to tell these teachers that this was the case.

In my classes now, I never aim to embarrass a student like that. Many of those teachers probably never thought I cried over that kind of embarrassment in private. Our actions can really hurt other people. I am always especially sympathetic to the anxious ones, I love them dearly. I myself am always anxious when I teach a class. It is scary to be in front of 30 or more people and act like you know what you are talking about. You have to be consistent, fun, and have an outgoing kind of personality. Sometimes, I am not those things and I cannot even pretend to be even if I wanted to.

I want you to know that if you have anxiety, I will always work something out with you. Sometimes, it is enough to do these exercises alone in your own room. At other times, it might be encouraging for you to imagine what it would be like to do this exercise and creatively write about this experience as you answer the questions. You might also try and bring some friends along with you as you try to do the exercises. I find that having friends with me sometimes helps alleviate some of the initial anxiety that I have.

I will talk with you more about this in private (if you are comfortable enough with me) and we can figure something out. I am always willing to help you out in any way I possibly can. But please remember that it is okay to feel anxious when doing these exercises!

8. What if for some reason I cannot do one of the exercises? Will I then not be sociological enough? Why do I have to do these exercises?

I have pretty much answered these questions above in various places. I will just concisely put them down here for reader convenience.

If you cannot do one of the exercises, there is always the possibility of creatively writing your experience and answering the questions that go along with the exercise. You can imagine yourself doing the exercise. While doing this, please feel free to be as visual as possible. You can time yourself for 10 minutes or so and try and imagine yourself somewhere doing the exercise. Or you can imagine someone else doing the exercise and observe them doing it. And of course, you can think of a time when you observed someone (including yourself) doing this exercise (perhaps unintentional or not) and record your experience of it. Another good way is to possibly ask a student or friend if you can observe them doing the exercise. And you can practice unobtrusive measures and record what happens. There are many ways that you can do the exercise without actually *doing* it.

Do not worry, anything you do with me in this course will automatically make you more sociological. I also have confidence in your abilities. The joy of journaling, exercising, and answering the focus questions will be our guides upon this sociological journey of ours.

The exercises are another way to understand these ideas. I think it is good to play on people's strong points. As I said earlier, some people can just read a text and instantaneously understand what has been said. Other people might have to go out and actually do it! Still others will find themselves in a better place if they read, do the exercises, and answer the focus questions. And others might find that "writing down their own experience" is the actual enlightening factor for them. And finally, there are some who just receive instant enlightenment upon hearing me explain what these things are! They all work together in harmony and each has its own place. I am merely bestowing a place for everyone to meet up at.

Hopefully, we can all make friends and enjoy each other's company on this brief sojourn of ours. May we work together to become more socially conscious. *Bon voyage* my friends!

APPENDIX 1

Let us look briefly at a map of our travels:

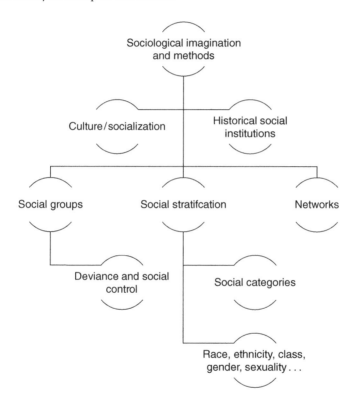

BIBLIOGRAPHY & READING LIST

Berger, Peter L. *Invitation to Sociology*. New York: Anchor Books, 1963. Print.

Garfinkel, Harold. *Studies in Ethnomethodology*. New Jersey: Prentice-Hall, 1967. Print.

Goffman, Irving. *Interaction Ritual*. New York: Pantheon Books, 1967. Print.

Goffman, Irving. *Symbolic Interaction*. Philadelphia: University of Pennsylvania Press, 1969. Print.

Goffman, Irving. *The Presentation of Self in Everyday Life*. New York: The Overlook Press, 1973. Print.

Kimmel, Michael S.; Ferber, Abby L. *Privilege: a Reader*. Colorado: Westview Press, 2014. Print.

Marx, Karl. *The Communist Manifesto*. New York: W. W. Norton & Company, 2013. Print.

McGrane, Bernard. *The Un-TV and the 10 MPH Car*. California: The Small Press, 1994. Print.

Mead, George Herbert. *The Individual and the Social Self*. Chicago: University of Chicago Press, 1982. Print.

Merton, Robert K. *Social Theory and Social Structure*. Illinois: The Free Press of Glencoe, 1963. Print.

Mills, C. Wright. *The Power Elite*. New York: Oxford University Press, 1956. Print.

Mills, C. Wright. *The Sociological Imagination*. New York: Oxford University Press, 1959. Print.

Park, Robert E. *The Crowd and the Public*. Chicago: University of Chicago Press, 1972. Print.

Rothenberg, Paula S. *White Privilege*. New York: Worth Publishers, 2008. Print.

Simmel, Georg. *On Individuality and Social Forms*. Chicago: University of Chicago Press, 1971. Print.

Simmel, Georg. *The Philosophy of Money*. New York: Routledge, 1978. Print.

Thomas, W. I. *On Social Organization and Social Personality*. Chicago: University of Chicago Press, 1966. Print.

Turner, Bryan S. *The Cambridge Dictionary of Sociology*. New York: Cambridge University Press, 2006. Print.

Webb, Eugene J.; Campbell, Donald T.; Schwartz, Richard D.; Sechrest, Lee. *Unobtrusive Measures: Nonreactive Research in the Social Sciences*. Chicago: Rand McNally & Company, 1966. Print.

Weber, Max. *The Protestant Ethic and the Spirit of Capitalism*. New York: W. W. Norton & Company, 2009. Print.

Wolff, Kurt H. *The Sociology of Georg Simmel*. London: The Free Press, 1950. Print.